Collins Road Atlas France

Contents

Driving in France

French drivers tend to be quite aggressive and the high incidence of road deaths has become a cause for national concern. There are speed restrictions for drivers who have held their licence for less than 2 years (110 km/h on motorways, 100 km/h on dual carriageways and 80 km/h on ordinary roads). Seatbelts are compulsory for both front and rear. Children under 10 should travel in the back, if possible. Babies and young children should be restrained appropriately, with a booster seat (**siège réhausseur**) or babyseat (**siège pour bébés**).

▲ **All routes**

▲ **Town centre**

built up area	50 km/h
ordinary roads	90 km/h
dual carriageway	110 km/h
motorway	130 km/h

▲ **Speed restrictions**

Motorways

Primary routes

Local routes

Temporary routes

Places of interest

▲ **French road signs are colour-coded**

▼ **Route for heavy vehicles**

▲ **Other routes**

NORTH	**Nord**		
WEST	**Ouest**	**Est**	EAST
	Sud	SOUTH	

▲ **Direction indicators**

Talking

we are going to...
nous allons à...
nooz a-loñ a...

is the road good?
est-ce que la route est bonne?
ess kuh la root ay bon

is the pass open?
est-ce que le col est ouvert?
ess kuh luh kol ayt oo-vehr

which is the best route?
quel est le meilleur itinéraire?
kel ay luh may-yuhr ee-tee-nay-rehr

can you show me on the map?
pouvez-vous me montrer sur la carte?
poo-vay voo muh moñ-tray soor la kart

do we need snow chains?
est-ce qu'il faut des chaînes?
ess keel foh day shen

◄ Lorry exit

▼ School exit

▲ Road liable to flooding

▲ Danger

▲ You do not have **priority.** The traffic on the roundabout has priority.

▲ Give way

Warning that the crossroads (**carrefour**) is a roundabout (in France roundabouts are ▼ fairly new).

▲ Slow down

▲ Detour

Road closed ▲

Follow the yellow detour signs to rejoin your route.

▲ Signs on entering
▼ and leaving town

is this the road to...?
c'est bien la route de...?
say byañ la root duh...

I am sorry, I did not know
je suis désolé, je ne savais pas
zhuh swee day-zo-lay zhuh nuh sa-vay pa

do I have to pay the fine straight away?
est-ce qu'il faut payer l'amende tout de suite?
ess keel foh pay-ay la-moñd toot sweet

how do I get to...?
pour aller à...?
poor a-lay a...

Although some portions of motorways are free around cities, you have to pay a toll if travelling over long distances. You get a ticket when you join the motorway. On leaving it you hand the ticket in at the **station péage** and the amount to pay is flashed up on an illuminated sign. Remember it is the front passenger who pays if you have a right-hand-drive car. Take care over speeding: limits are lowered in wet weather – by 20 km/h on motorways and 10 km/h on other roads.

▲ **Motorway emergency phone**

▲ **Motorway signs are blue; local signs are white**

▼ **Motorway junction/exit**

The motorway routes sign posted here
▼ are toll-paying (**péage**).

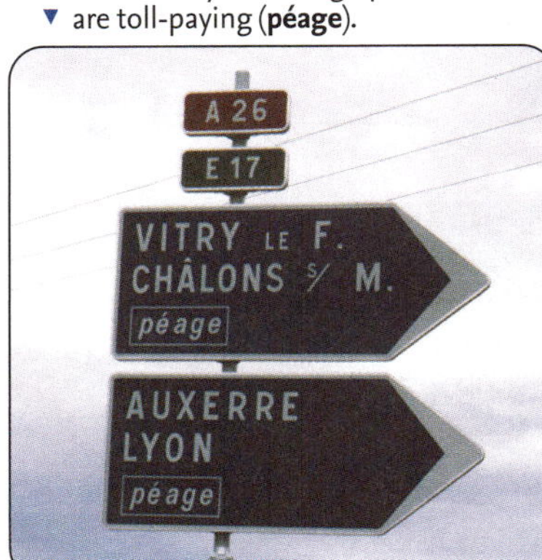

▲ **Toll station**

◄ **Stop**
Toll station

▼ **Motorway services are located every 30–40 km**

If you break down on the motorway

If you break down on the motorway, first you should put on your hazard lights and place the warning triangle about 30 m behind the car. You should alert the police on emergency number 17 stating your exact location. If you are using an emergency SOS phone (located every 2 km along the motorway) they will know your location. The police will arrange for a recovery vehicle to come to you.

my car has broken down
ma voiture est en panne
ma vwa-toor ay oñ pan

what do I do?
qu'est-ce que je dois faire?
kess kuh zhuh dwa fehr

I am on my own (female)
je suis seule
zhuh swee suhl

my children are in the car
mes enfants sont dans la voiture
mayz oñ-foñ soñ doñ la vwa-toor

the car is near junction number...
la voiture est près de la sortie numéro...
la vwa-toor ay pray duh la sor-tee noo-may-roh...

it's a blue Fiat Uno
c'est une Fiat Uno bleue
say ooñ fyat oo-noh bluh

registration number...
numéro d'immatriculation...
noo-may-roh dee-mat-ree-koo-las-yoñ...

In Paris, you generally pay to park. Outside Paris, in some parts of many towns, parking is only allowed on one side of the road. The system is that for the first 15 days of the month, parking is on the side of the road with odd house-numbers. During the second half of the month, parking is on the even-numbered-house side.

◂ **Pay at the meter** (below the sign).

Paying

▾ Most of the time, parking is not free.

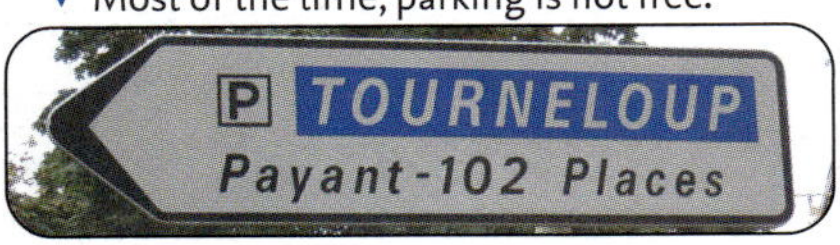

▴ **Only 3 minutes**

▾ **Parking meter**

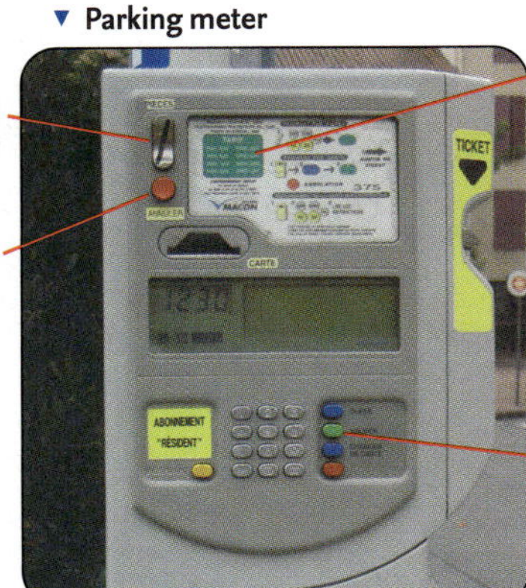

▴ **No parking on the pavement**

no parking

vehicle exit

▲ Newer parking machines take notes and let you choose the language for your transaction.

▲ No parking on Saturdays, market day

▲ Don't be fooled: **libre** means there are spaces, not that parking is free.

▲ **Car park full**

▲ **Open 24 hours**

▲
Disabled parking places
▼

I am looking for a car park
je cherche un parking
zhuh shehrsh uñ par-keeng

can I park here?
est-ce que je peux me garer ici?
ess kuh zhuh puh muh ga-ray ee-see

the ticket machine doesn't work
l'horodateur ne marche pas
lo-ro-da-tuhr nuh marsh pa

do I need to pay?
il faut payer?
eel foh pay-ay

how long for?
pour combien de temps?
poor koñ-byañ duh toñ

Petrol stations in small towns are generally manned, but closed Sundays and in the evenings. The big towns have 24-hour petrol stations and you can buy petrol at some large supermarkets.

◄ **Petrol pumps are colour-coded** You will find the pump number at the side

◄ Colour-coding matches the pump handle: green for unleaded (**sans plomb**), blue for super and yellow for diesel. The figure to the right (98, 95, 97) refers to the octane rating. Most cars run on the lower rating. The higher one is for powerful cars or towing cars.

◄ Diesel is also known as **gazoil** or **gazole**.

◄ **Turn off engine**

Talking

is there a petrol station near here?
est-ce qu'il y a une station-service près d'ici?
ess keel ee a oon stass-yoñ sehr-vees pray dee-see

fill it up please
le plein s'il vous plaît
luh plañ see voo play

40 euro worth of unleaded petrol
quarante euro d'essence sans plomb
ka-roñt uh-roh dess-oñss soñ ploñ

I'd like to wash the car
je voudrais laver la voiture
zhuh voo-dray la-vay la vwa-toor

pump number...
pompe numéro...
poñp noo-may-roh...

how much is that?
c'est combien?
say koñ-byañ

You should carry a red warning triangle in case of breakdown. It is also advisable to carry a first-aid kit in the car. You will have no trouble in France finding a **garage** to do repairs.

I have broken down
je suis en panne
zhuh swee oñ pan

I have a flat tyre
j'ai un pneu crevé
zhay uñ pnuh kruh-vay

I need tyres
j'ai besoin de pneus
zhay buh-zwañ duh pnuh

where is the nearest garage?
où est le garage le plus proche?
oo ay luh ga-razh luh ploo prosh

the ... is not working
le/la ... ne marche pas
luh/la ... nuh marsh pa

can you repair it?
vous pouvez le réparer?
voo poo-vay luh ray-pa-ray

when will it be ready?
ça sera prêt quand?
sa suh-ra pray koñ

can you replace the windscreen?
pouvez-vous changer le pare-brise?
poo-vay voo shoñ-zhay luh par-breez

the car won't start
la voiture ne démarre pas
la vwa-toor nuh day-mar pa

the battery is flat
la batterie est à plat
la ba-tree ayt a pla

I have run out of petrol
je suis en panne d'essence
zhuh swee oñ pan dess-oñss

something is wrong with...
il y a un problème avec...
eel ee a uñ pro-blehm a-vek...

the ... are not working
les ... ne marchent pas
lay ... nuh marsh pa

how long will it take?
ça va prendre combien de temps?
sa va proñdr koñ-byañ duh toñ

how much will it cost?
combien ça va coûter?
koñ-byañ sa va koo-tay

please check...
vous pouvez vérifier...
voo poo-vay ve-ree-fyay...

the oil
l'huile
lweel

the water
l'eau
loh

the tyres
les pneus
lay pnuh

Emergency

The emergency number is 17 for the police (15 for an ambulance and 18 for the fire brigade). You will see either **Police** or **Gendarmerie** (in smaller towns and villages). You should report all thefts or crimes to them.

▲ Fire station

▲ Local police

▲ Police station

help!
au secours!
oh suh-koor

can you help me?
vous pouvez m'aider?
voo poo-vay mah-day

please call...
s'il vous plaît! appelez...
seel voo play ap-lay...

the police
la police
la po-leess

an ambulance
une ambulance
oon oñ-boo-loñss

fire!
au feu!
oh fuh

please call the fire brigade!
s'il vous plaît! appelez les pompiers!
seel voo play ap-lay lay poñ-pyay

my ... has been stolen
on m'a volé mon/ma...
oñ ma vo-lay moñ/ma...

I want to report a theft
je veux signaler un vol
zhuh vuh seen-ya-lay uñ vol

here are my insurance details
voici mon assurance
vwa-see moñ a-soo-roñss

please give me your insurance details
votre assurance s'il vous plaît
votr a-soo-roñss seel voo play

where is the police station?
où est la gendarmerie?
oo ay la zhoñ-darm-ree

I would like to phone...
je voudrais appeler...
zhuh voo-dray ap-lay...

my car has been broken into
on a forcé ma voiture
on a for-say ma vwa-toor

I need a report for my insurance
il me faut un constat pour mon assurance
eel muh foh uñ koñ-sta poor mon a-soo-roñss

Regional map of France

▼ Tourist information

French Tourist Office
178 Piccadilly
London
W1J 9AL

Web address: www.franceguide.com
Tel. no.: 0906 8 244 123

Capital city: **Paris**

▼ Country identification

- AND Andorra
- B Belgium
- CH Switzerland
- D Germany
- E Spain
- F France
- GB United Kingdom GB & NI
- GBA Alderney
- GBG Guernsey
- GBJ Jersey
- I Italy
- L Luxembourg
- MC Monaco

▼ Internet links

Tourist information	Motoring information
www.franceguide.com	www.asecap.com
www.fco.gov.uk	www.autoroutes.fr
www.met-office.gov.uk	www.drive-alive.co.uk/distances.htm
www.bbc.co.uk/weather	www.drive-alive.co.uk/autoroutes.htm

Distance chart

	Amiens	Bordeaux	Brest	Calais	Cherbourg	Clermont-Ferrand	Dijon	Grenoble	Le Havre	Lyon	Marseille	Nantes	Nice	PARIS	Perpignan	Reims	Rennes	Strasbourg	Toulouse
Bordeaux	725																		
Brest	616	628																	
Calais	161	890	714																
Cherbourg	359	654	394	457															
Clermont-Ferrand	568	381	788	729	656														
Dijon	481	709	833	582	650	287													
Grenoble	776	655	1076	883	912	274	301												
Le Havre	176	639	464	274	207	560	521	763											
Lyon	667	546	953	768	797	165	186	109	648										
Marseille	968	700	1229	1069	1098	441	487	272	949	291									
Nantes	501	345	283	629	309	474	619	748	379	639	1045								
Nice	1130	866	1391	1231	1260	603	649	313	1131	453	203	1211							
PARIS	147	560	559	290	337	421	313	575	188	460	761	387	923						
Perpignan	1136	485	1113	1159	1109	430	638	457	990	460	333	830	499	851					
Reims	166	712	757	267	481	565	315	616	342	501	802	531	964	144	953				
Rennes	420	444	230	530	210	573	561	861	280	738	1054	99	1220	329	929	473			
Strasbourg	521	1007	1065	629	843	567	328	566	697	486	788	893	751	504	956	360	833		
Toulouse	832	252	880	993	876	379	666	572	824	575	448	597	614	685	233	829	696	1071	
Tours	380	334	458	540	364	332	398	606	309	493	773	211	935	226	762	382	232	673	489

Distances in kilometres.
The distances given in this chart are obtained by following main routes and are not necessarily the shortest routes.

Key to map pages

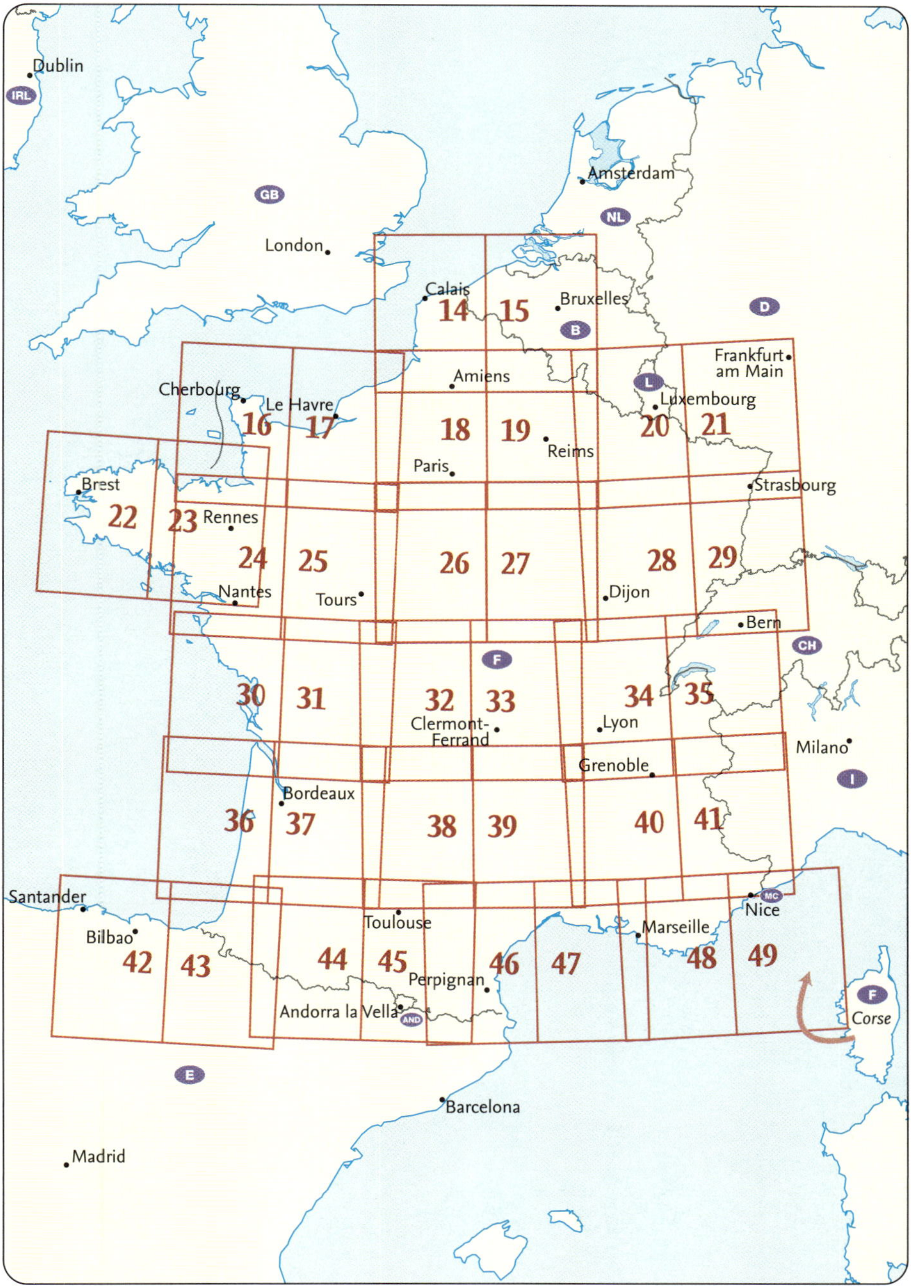

1
2
3
A
B
C
D
GB
F
17
18
Margate
Herne Bay
Birchington
Whitstable
North Foreland
Broadstairs
Ramsgate
Sarre
Pegwell Bay
Sturry
Sandwich
Canterbury
Eastry
Deal
Barham
Walmer
Wye
Temple Ewell
Whitfield
South Foreland
Hawkinge
Dover
Hythe
Folkestone
Romney Marsh
Dymchurch
Littlestone-on-Sea
Dungeness
Great Stour
Channel Tunnel
Strait of Dover
(Pas de Calais)
Oostende
(Ostend)
Middelkerke
Nieuwpoort
Koksijde
De Panne
Veurne
Diksmuide
St-Pol-sur-Mer
Dunkerque
Grande-Synthe
Coudekerque-Branche
Ghyvelde
Hondschoote
Grand-Fort-Philippe
Gravelines
Bergues
Oostvleteren
Houthulst
Calais
Sangatte
Marck
Cap Blanc Nez
Bourbourg
Coulogne
Wissant
Guînes
Audruicq
Wormhout
Poperinge
Ieper
Langemark
Cap Gris Nez
Ardres
Audresselles
Marquise
Watten
Steenvoorde
Dikkebus
Ambleteuse
Licques
Cassel
Mont des Cats
Kemmelberg
Kemmel
Wimereux
St-Omer
Arques
Bailleul
St-Martin-Boulogne
Boulogne-sur-Mer
Longuenesse
Le Portel
Outreau
Lumbres
Wizernes
Hazebrouck
Armentières
Desvres
Hardelot-Plage
Neufchâtel-Hardelot
Samer
Thérouanne
Aire-sur-la-Lys
Merville
Estaires
Isbergues
Fauquembergues
Norrent-Fontes
Canal d'Aire
Lillers
Hucqueliers
Frencq
Collines de l'Artois
Auchy-au-Bois
Béthune
La Bassée
Le Touquet-Paris-Plage
Étaples
Montcavrel
Fruges
Beuvry
Heuchin
Bruay-la-Bussière
Montreuil
Lebiez
Divion
Nœux-les-Mines
Anvin
Houdain
Bully-les-Mines
Avion
Lens
Berck
Canche
Verton
Campagne-lès-Hesdin
Hesdin
Le Parcq
St-Pol-sur-Ternoise
Aubigny-en-Artois
Vimy
Fort-Mahon-Plage
Quend
Authie
Vron
Douriez
TERNOIS
St-Nicolas
Arras
Dainville
Rue
Frévent
Avesnes-le-Comte
Achicourt
Baie de la Somme
Pte du Hourdel
Le Crotoy
Crécy-en-Ponthieu
Nouvion
Auxi-le-Château
Beaumetz-lès-Loges
Cayeux-sur-Mer
St-Valery-sur-Somme
PONTHIEU
Lucheux
Pas-en-Artois
Ervillers
St-Riquier
Bernaville
Doullens
Ault
Friville-Escarbotin
Cambron
Abbeville
Ailly-le-Haut-Clocher
Beauval
Puisieux
Bapaume
Mers-les-Bains
Le Tréport
Moyenneville
Beauquesne
Long
Domart-en-Ponthieu
Canaples
Acheux-en-Amiénois
Mailly-Maillet
Newhaven
Criel-sur-Mer
Eu
Feuquières-en-Vimeu
St-Ouen
Penly
Incheville
VIMEU
Flixecourt
Vignacourt
Warloy-Baillon
Albert
Combles
Gamaches
Hallencourt
Airaines
Villers-Bocage
Méaulte
Dieppe
Neuville-lès-Dieppe
Blangy-sur-Bresle
Oisemont
Picquigny
Amiens
Querrieu
Bray-sur-Somme
Offranville
Arques-la-Bataille
Envermeu
Senarpont
Ailly-sur-Somme
Rivery
Corbie
Camon
Longueau
Fouilloy
Villers-Bretonneux
Carbonnel
Fresnoy-Folny
Molliens-Dreuil
Salouël
St-Nicolas-d'Aliermont
Beaucamps-le-Vieux
Londinières
Foucarmont
Hornoy-le-Bourg
Boves
Rosières-en-Santerre
Chaulnes
Béthune
Longueville-sur-Scie
PICARDIE
FLANDRE
A28
A299
A253
A257
A2
A256
A258
A260
A20
A259
A16
A26
A25
A18
E40
E402
E15
E44
A28
A29
A1
N1
N42
N43
N39
N25
N17
N41
N47
N50
N225
N365
D916
D928
D925
D929

NL
B
Vlissingen
Middelburg
Goes
Bergen op Zoom
Roosendaal
Breda
Oosterhout
Oosterschelde
Westerschelde
Terneuzen
Hulst
Knokke-Heist
Zeebrugge
Brugge (Bruges)
Oostkamp
Maldegem
Eeklo
Zelzate
Sas Van Gent
Antwerpen (Anvers)
Schoten
Brasschaat
Kapellen
Mortsel
Boechout
Lier
Herentals
Geel
St-Niklaas
Lokeren
Temse
Hamme
Gent (Gand)
Melle
Merelbeke
Wetteren
Dendermonde
Aalst (Alost)
Mechelen (Malines)
Vilvoorde
Zaventem
Leuven (Louvain)
Aarschot
Diest
Tienen
BRUXELLES (BRUSSEL)
Schaerbeek
Anderlecht
Ixelles
Uccle
Halle
Waterloo
Wavre
Tielt
Roeselare
Izegem
Kortrijk (Courtrai)
Waregem
Oudenaarde
Ninove
Geraardsbergen
Zottegem
Mouscron
Tourcoing
Roubaix
Lille
Villeneuve-d'Ascq
Tournai
Ath
Lessines
Enghien
Soignies
Braine-le-Comte
Nivelles
Mons
La Louvière
St-Ghislain
BORINAGE
Charleroi
Fleurus
Gembloux
Namur
Valenciennes
Denain
Maubeuge
Cambrai
Caudry
Le Cateau-Cambrésis
Avesnes-sur-Helpe
Fourmies
Hirson
St-Quentin
Guise
Chimay
Philippeville
Dinant
Givet
HAINAUT
VERMANDOIS
THIÉRACHE
Fagne
L'Eau d'Heure
Forêt de Nismes
Bois de Chimay
Sambre
Oise
Meuse
E19
E17
E40
E42
E34
E403
E411
E429
E313
E312
E420
E44
A1
A2
A4
A7
A8
A10
A12
A14
A15
A16
A17
A23
A26
A27
A54
A58
4
5
6
A
B
C
D
19

1
2
3
A
B
C
D
Weymouth
Poole
Portsmouth
Portsmouth
Portsmouth
Dublin, Rosslare
E N G L I S H
L A M
BAIE
Alderney
St Anne
GBA
Cap de la Hague
Auderville
Urville Nacqueville
Beaumont
Équeurdreville-Hainneville
Octeville
Cherbourg
Tourlaville
La Glacerie
Cap Lévy
Pte de Barfleur
Barfleur
St-Pierre-Église
Quettehou
Guernsey
Vale
St Sampson
GBG
Herm
St Peter Port
St Martin
Torteval
Sark
CHANNEL ISLANDS
Flamanville
Les Pieux
Brix
Valognes
Montebourg
Îles St-Marcouf
Bricquebec
COTENTIN
Ste-Mère-Église
St-Sauveur-le-Vicomte
Carteret
Barneville-Carteret
Cap de Carteret
Portbail
Picauville
Grandcamp-Maisy
Vierville-sur-Mer
Port-en-Bessin-Huppain
Isigny-sur-Mer
Trévières
Passage de la Déroute
GBJ
Jersey
St John
St Ouen
St Martin
St Brelade
St Saviour
St Helier
St Clement
La Haye-du-Puits
St-Jores
Carentan
BESSIN
Bayeux
Lessay
St-Jean-de-Daye
Le Molay-Littry
Vaubadon
Créances
Périers
Tribehou
Cerisy-la-Forêt
Balleroy
Pont-Hébert
St-Sauveur-Lendelin
St-Lô
Marigny
Agneaux
St-Malo-de-la-Lande
Blainville-sur-Mer
Agon-Coutainville
Caumont-l'Eventé
Condé-sur-Vire
Coutances
Cerisy-la-Salle
Torigni-sur-Vire
Les Minquiers
St-Martin-des-Besaces
Montmartin-sur-Mer
Quettreville-sur-Sienne
Tessy-sur-Vire
23
Hambye
Percy
Pont-Farcy
Îles Chausey
Bréhal
Cérences
Gavray
BOCAGE
Villedieu-les-Poêles
St-Sever-Calvados
Donville-les-Bains
Granville
Vire
St-Pair-sur-Mer
La Haye-Pesnel
Golfe de St-Malo
Jullouville
Sartilly
St-Pois
Collines
Carolles
Tinchebray
Brécey
Pte du Grouin
Cap Fréhel
Rothéneuf
Cancale
Baie du Mont-St-Michel
Genêts
Sourdeval
Sables-d'Or-les-Pins
Erquy
Fréhel
Dinard
Paramé
St-Lunaire
St-Malo
St-Méloir-des-Ondes
Le Vivier-sur-Mer
Avranches
Juvigny-le-Tertre
Mortain
Pontaubault
Ducey
Pléneuf-Val-André
St-Briac-sur-Mer
St-Jouan-des-Guérets
Matignon
Ploubalay
Châteauneuf-d'Ille-et-Vilaine
Pontorson
Sélune
St-Hilaire-du-Harcouët
Barenton
Hénanbihen
Plancoët
Dol-de-Bretagne
Pleine-Fougères
St-James
St-Martin-de-Landelles
Le Teilleul
Miniac-Morvan
Argouges
Louvigné-du-Désert
Buais
Landivy
Lamballe
Pleudihen-sur-Rance
Trans
Corseul
Dinan
Cuguen
St-Pierre-de-Plesguen
St-Brice-en-Coglès
Fougerolles-du-Plessis
Gorron
Maroué
Léhon
Meillac
Combourg
24
Montaudin
Plénée-Jugon
Jugon-les-Lacs
Évran
Dingé
Romazy
Lécousse
Larchamp
Châtillon-sur-Colmont
Yvignac
THIÈVRE

4
5
6
14
CHANNEL
NCHE
E SEINE
Newhaven
A
B
C
D
18
25
Dieppe
Neuville-lès-Dieppe
Mers-les-Bains
Le Tréport
Criel-sur-Mer
Penly
Varengeville-sur-Mer
Offranville
Arques-la-Bataille
St-Valery-en-Caux
Veulettes-sur-Mer
St-Pierre-en-Port
Paluel
Néville
Bourg-Dun
Fontaine-le-Dun
Bacqueville-en-Caux
Cany-Barville
Longueville-sur-Scie
Fécamp
Yport
Valmont
Étretat
Cap d'Antifer
St-Jouin-Bruneval
Criquetot-l'Esneval
Fauville-en-Caux
Goderville
Ourville-en-Caux
Doudeville
St-Laurent-en-Caux
Auffay
Bellencombre
Tôtes
St-Saëns
PAYS DE CAUX
Yerville
Yvetot
Clères
Pavilly
Barentin
Montville
Malaunay
Fontaine-le-Bourg
Mont-St-Aignan
Villers-Écalles
Bois-Guillaume
Rouen
Maromme
Le Petit-Quevilly
Le Grand-Quevilly
Sotteville-lès-Rouen
Grand-Couronne
St-Étienne-du-Rouvray
Oissel
Duclair
Octeville-sur-Mer
Montivilliers
Cap de la Hève
Ste-Adresse
Harfleur
Le Havre
Gonfreville-l'Orcher
Tancarville
Bolbec
Lillebonne
Notre-Dame-de-Gravenchon
Quillebeuf-sur-Seine
Seine
Honfleur
Villerville
Trouville-sur-Mer
Deauville
Beuzeville
Pont-Audemer
Routot
Bourg-Achard
St-Aubin-lès-Elbeuf
Elbeuf
Cléon
Caudebec-lès-Elbeuf
Bourgtheroulde-Infreville
St-Pierre-lès-Elbeuf
Louviers
Montfort-sur-Risle
Courseulles-sur-Mer
St-Aubin-sur-Mer
Luc-sur-Mer
Lion-sur-Mer
Villers-sur-Mer
Houlgate
Dives-sur-Mer
Douvres-la-Délivrande
Ouistreham
Touques
Pont-l'Évêque
Cormeilles
Épaignes
St-Georges-du-Vièvre
Le Gros Theil
Brionne
Le Neubourg
Hérouville-St-Clair
Mondeville
Colombelles
Carpiquet
Caen
Verson
Dozulé
Troarn
Argences
Moult
Mézidon-Canon
Lisieux
Thiberville
Bernay
Serquigny
Quittebeuf
Acquigny
Gaillon
Ifs
Bourguébus
Évrecy
Brettville-sur-Laize
St-Sylvain
PAYS D'AUGE
Livarot
Orbec
Broglie
Beaumont-le-Roger
St-Sébastien-de-Morsent
Évreux
Gravigny
La Bonneville-sur-Iton
Conches-en-Ouche
Thury-Harcourt
Potigny
St-Pierre-sur-Dives
Beaumesnil
NORMANDIE
Vimoutiers
La Barre-en-Ouche
La Neuve-Lyre
St-André-de-l'Eure
Clécy
Pont-d'Ouilly
Falaise
Morteaux-Coulibœuf
PAYS D'OUCHE
Glos-la-Ferrière
Breteuil
Damville
SUISSE NORMANDE
Trun
La Ferté-Frênel
Rugles
Marcilly-sur-Eure
Athis-de-l'Orne
Bazoches-au-Houlme
Chambois
Exmes
Gacé
St-Sulpice-sur-Risle
Nonancourt
St-Lubin-des-Joncherets
St-Georges-des-Groseillers
Putanges-Pont-Écrepin
Argentan
Écouché
Le Pin-au-Haras
L'Aigle
Aube
Verneuil-sur-Avre
Tillières-sur-Avre
Messei
Briouze
Échauffour
Brézolles
Laons
Bellou-en-Houlme
Bouçé
Le Merlerault
Moulins-la-Marche
Randonnai
La Ferté-Vidame
Maillebois
Rânes
Mortrée
Courtomer
Tourouvre
Châteauneuf-en-Thymerais
La Ferté-Macé
Sées
Bazoches-sur-Hoëne
Longny-au-Perche
Senonches
Carrouges
Le Mêle-sur-Sarthe
Mortagne-au-Perche
Belhomert-Guéhouville
Digny
Couterne
Essay
Campagne d'Alençon
Collines du Perche
Couptrain
Pré-en-Pail
Damigny
Alençon
Pervenchères
Le Pin-la-Garenne
Rémalard
La Loupe
Courville-sur-Eure
Javron-les-Chapelles
Mont des Avaloirs
St-Germain-du-Corbéis
Bretoncelles
Le Horps
St-Pierre-des-Nids
Arçonnay
Mamers
Bellême
Nocé
Condé-sur-Huisne
Bailleau-le-Pin
Eure
Orne
Béthune
Mayenne

Baie de la Somme
Pte du Hourdel
Le Crotoy
Cayeux-sur-Mer
St-Valery-sur-Somme
PONTHIEU
Crécy-en-Ponthieu
Nouvion
Abbeville
St-Riquier
Auxi-le-Château
Frévent
14
Doullens
Lucheux
Pas-en-Artois
Avesnes-le-Comte
Beaumetz-lès-Loges
Dainville
Achicourt
Croisil
Ervillers
Bapaume
Puisieux
Mailly-Maillet
Albert
Combles
Méaulte
Bray-sur-Somme
Acheux-en-Amiénois
Beauquesne
Beauval
Bernaville
Canaples
Domart-en-Ponthieu
St-Ouen
Vignacourt
Villers-Bocage
Warloy-Baillon
Ailly-le-Haut-Clocher
Long
Flixecourt
Airaines
Hallencourt
Oisemont
Senarpont
VIMEU
Moyenneville
Cambron
Friville-Escarbotin
Ault
Mers-les-Bains
Le Tréport
Eu
Feuquières-en-Vimeu
Gamaches
Incheville
Criel-sur-Mer
Penly
Newhaven
Dieppe
Neuville-lès-Dieppe
Arques-la-Bataille
Envermeu
St-Nicolas-d'Aliermont
Londinières
Blangy-sur-Bresle
Fresnoy-Folny
Foucarmont
Beaucamps-le-Vieux
Molliens-Dreuil
Picquigny
Ailly-sur-Somme
Amiens
Rivery
Camon
Longueau
Salouël
Saleux
Boves
Querrieu
Corbie
Fouilloy
Villers-Bretonneux
Rosières-en-Santerre
Chaulnes
Villers-Carbonnel
Hornoy-le-Bourg
Quevauvillers
Poix-de-Picardie
Conty
Ailly-sur-Noye
Moreuil
Bouchoir
Roye
PICARDIE
SANTERRE
Aumale
Longueville-sur-Scie
Auffay
Bellencombre
Tôtes
St-Saëns
Neufchâtel-en-Bray
Formerie
Grandvilliers
Crèvecœur-le-Grand
Feuquières
Forges-les-Eaux
Clères
Montville
Malaunay
Fontaine-le-Bourg
Buchy
Argueil
Marseille-en-Beauvaisis
Songeons
Luchy
Breteuil
Montdidier
Tricot
Lassigny
Froissy
Maignelay-Montigny
Ressons-sur-Matz
St-Just-en-Chaussée
Gournay-en-Bray
Mont-St-Aignan
Bois-Guillaume
Rouen
Sotteville-lès-Rouen
St-Étienne-du-Rouvray
Boos
Fleury-sur-Andelle
Lyons-la-Forêt
Troissereux
Beauvais
Nivillers
Le Coudray-St-Germer
Sérifontaine
Clermont
Fitz-James
Estrées-St-Denis
Clairoix
Compiègne
Liancourt
Verberie
VEXIN NORMAND
Pîtres
Elbeuf
Caudebec-lès-Elbeuf
Val-de-Reuil
St-Pierre-lès-Elbeuf
Écouis
Étrépagny
Trie-Château
Gisors
Chaumont-en-Vexin
Noailles
Ste-Geneviève
Mouy
Pont-Ste-Maxence
Nogent-sur-Oise
Creil
Pontpoint
Crépy-en-Valois
Louviers
Les Andelys
Bouafles
Tourny
Méru
Neuilly-en-Thelle
Montataire
Senlis
Chantilly
Gouvieux
Acquigny
Gaillon
VEXIN FRANÇAIS
Écos
Magny-en-Vexin
Marines
Amblainville
Persan
Beaumont-sur-Oise
Viarmes
Ermenonville
Nanteuil-le-Haudouin
Quittebeuf
Vernon
St-Marcel
Gasny
L'Isle-Adam
Luzarches
Dammartin-en-Goële
Le Plessis-Belleville
St-Soupplets
Évreux
Gravigny
Pacy-sur-Eure
Vétheuil
Vigny
Osny
Pontoise
Domont
Goussainville
Morsent
Mantes-la-Jolie
Limay
Cergy
Taverny
Sarcelles
Mantes-la-Ville
Meulan
Les Mureaux
Argenteuil
St-Denis
Mitry-Mory
Conches-en-Ouche
Breuilpont
Plaine de St-André
St-André-de-l'Eure
Aubergenville
Poissy
Aulnay-sous-Bois
St-Germain-en-Laye
Le Raincy
Lagny-sur-Marne
Damville
La Couture-Boussey
Ézy-sur-Eure
Ivry-la-Bataille
Septeuil
Thoiry
Rueil-Malmaison
Nanterre
Boulogne-Billancourt
PARIS
Marne-la-Vallée
Anet
Plaisir
Ivry-sur-Seine
Marcilly-sur-Eure
St-Lubin-des-Joncherets
Nonancourt
Bû
Houdan
Versailles
Créteil
Pontault-Combault
Ozoir-la-Ferrière
Tournan-en-Brie
Tillières-sur-Avre
St-Rémy-sur-Avre
Montfort-l'Amaury
Trappes
Antony
Dreux
Laons
Vernouillet
Chevreuse
Palaiseau
Orsay
Montgeron
Brie-Comte-Robert
St-Léger-en-Yvelines
Coulombs
Forêt de Rambouillet
Rambouillet
Tréon
Tremblay-les-Villages
Nogent-le-Roi
Épernon
Maillebois
Châteauneuf-en-Thymerais
Évry
Corbeil-Essonnes
Guignes
Mormant
Pierres
Maintenon
St-Arnoult-en-Yvelines
HUREPOIX
Arpajon
Mennecy
Cesson
Melun
Thimert-Gâtelles
Digny
Gallardon
Jouy
Dourdan
Vaux-le-Pénil
Courville-sur-Eure
La Loupe
Mainvilliers
Lèves
Chartres
Lucé
Luisant
Ablis
Auneau
Béville-le-Comte
Étréchy
Étampes
26
La Ferté-Alais
Milly-la-Forêt
Perthes
Fontainebleau
Champagne-sur-Seine
Avon
Bailleau-le-Pin
Thivars
Sours
Sainville
Maisse
17
VALOIS
Eure
Seine
Oise
Béthune
Avre
A
B
C
D
1
2
3

H A I N A U T
Cambrai
Le Quesnoy
Hautmont
Walcourt
Florennes
Philippeville
Beaumont
L'Eau d'Heure
F a g n e
Solesmes
Le Cateau-Cambrésis
Landrecies
Avesnes-sur-Helpe
Caudry
Marcoing
Villers-Outréaux
Le Catelet
Bohain-en-Vermandois
Wassigny
Le Nouvion-en-Thiérache
La Capelle
Fourmies
Chimay
Couvin
Mariembourg
Nismes
Forêt de Nismes
Bois de Chimay
Givet
Beauraing
Vireux-Wallerand
Fumay
Hirson
Anor
Revin
Rocroi
V E R M A N D O I S
St-Quentin
Guise
Vervins
T H I É R A C H E
Aubenton
Signy-le-Petit
Maubert-Fontaine
Monthermé
Nouzonville
Vallée de la Meuse
Charleville-Mézières
Sedan
Rumigny
Liart
Rouvroy-sur-Audry
Ham
Tergnier
Chauny
La Fère
Marle
Montcornet
Rozoy-sur-Serre
Signy-l'Abbaye
Laon
Chambry
Crépy
St-Gobain
Sissonne
Dizy-le-Gros
Chaumont-Porcien
Novion-Porcien
P O R C I E N
Château-Porcien
Rethel
Poix-Terron
Omont
Tourteron
Le Chesne
Attigny
Vouziers
Grandpré
Soissons
Coucy-le-Château-Auffrique
Anizy-le-Château
Vailly-sur-Aisne
Craonne
Corbeny
Guignicourt
Neufchâtel-sur-Aisne
Asfeld
Juniville
Machault
Monthois
Braine
Fismes
Villers-Cotterêts
T A R D E N O I S
Reims
Tinqueux
Cormontreuil
Berru
Witry-lès-Reims
Pontfaverger-Moronvilliers
Sommepy-Tahure
Suippes
Ste-Menehould
Valmy
Mont Cornillet
Mémorial Américain
La Neuville-au-Pont
Ville-sur-Tourbe
Cernay-en-Dormois
Oulchy-le-Château
Fère-en-Tardenois
Neuilly-St-Front
Coincy
Ville-en-Tardenois
Châtillon-sur-Marne
Verzy
Mont Sinaï
Avenay-Val-d'Or
Dormans
Château-Thierry
La Ferté-sous-Jouarre
Épernay
Mareuil-sur-Ay
Avize
Oger
Le Mesnil-sur-Oger
Vertus
Bergères-lès-Vertus
Montmirail
Champaubert
Orbais-l'Abbaye
Montmort-Lucy
Châlons-en-Champagne
St-Memmie
Sarry
La Veuve
Tilloy-et-Bellay
Dommartin-Varimont
Givry-en-Argonne
Possesse
Vanault-les-Dames
Heiltz-le-Maurupt
Revigny-sur-Ornain
Coulommiers
La Ferté-Gaucher
Rebais
Le Gault-Soigny
Esternay
Sézanne
CÔTE CHAMPENOISE
Fère-Champenoise
Connantre
Sommesous
Vitry-le-François
CHAMPAGNE POUILLEUSE
PERTHOIS
St-Dizier
Provins
Villenauxe-la-Grande
Nogent-sur-Seine
Romilly-sur-Seine
Anglure
Méry-sur-Seine
Arcis-sur-Aube
Mailly-le-Camp
Lhuître
Nogent-sur-Aube
Margerie-Hancourt
Chavanges
Brienne-le-Château
Lac du Der Étang de la Horre
Montier-en-Der
Wassy
Bray-sur-Seine
Marigny-le-Châtel
Montsuzain
Lesmont
Dienville
Soulaines-Dhuys
Seine
Marne
Aisne
Oise
Vesle
Aube
Voire
Meuse

Marche-en-Famenne
Hotton
Baraque de Fraiture
Lierneux
Vielsalm
St-Vith
Haversin
Rochefort
Focant
Heer
Givet
Doische
Beauraing
Wellin
Tellin
Hargimont
Nassogne
La Roche-en-Ardenne
Tenneville
Bertogne
Houffalize
Bovigny
Gouvy
Thommen
Oudler
Troisvierges
Weiswampach
Bleialf
Prüm
Weinsheim
Gerolstein
Birresborn
Schönecken
Pronsfeld
Lünebach
Waxweiler
Arzfeld
Daleiden
Chooz
Vireux-Wallerand
Fépin
Hargnies
Fumay
Gedinne
Bièvre
Paliseul
St-Hubert
Libin
Amberloup
Bastogne
Wincrange
Clervaux
Hosingen
Neuerburg
Bitburg
Wiltz
Plateau de l'Ardenne
Vallée de la Semois
Vaux-sur-Sûre
Libramont
Hollange
Esch-sur-Sûre
Vianden
Körperich
Mettendorf
Bettingen
Vresse
Gespunsart
Nouzonville
Bertrix
Longlier
Neufchâteau
Martelange
Diekirch
Ettelbruck
Bettendorf
Schieren
Irrel
Ralingen
Welschbillig
Echternach
Monthermé
Montcy-Notre-Dame
Vivier-au-Court
Bouillon
Straimont
Léglise
Forêt d'Anlier
Redange
Rambrouch
Bissen
Berg
Larochette
Forêt de Chiny
Rossignol
Florenville
Tintigny
Habay-la-Neuve
Attert
Saeul
Mersch
Junglinster
Mertert
Grevenmacher
Sedan
Balan
Floing
La Chapelle
Donchery
Flize
Messincourt
Carignan
Douzy
Mouzon
GAUME
Étalle
Châtillon
Arlon
Steinfort
Kehlen
Capellen
Walferdange
Niederanven
Nittel
Wormeldange
Saarburg
Serrig
Poix-Terron
Omont
Chémery-sur-Bar
Meix-devant-Virton
Avioth
Virton
St-Léger
Ethe
Aubange
Clémency
Mamer
Strassen
Dippach
LUXEMBOURG
Hesperange
Margut
Montmédy
Musson
Mont-St-Martin
Longwy
Pétange
Bascharage
Sanem
Bettembourg
Frisange
Remich
Palzem
Tannay
Beaumont-en-Argonne
Laneuville-sur-Meuse
Stenay
Le Chesne
Baâlon
Tellancourt
Velosnes
Marville
Differdange
Esch-sur-Alzette
Schifflange
Mondorf-les-Bains
Perl
Borg
Quatre-Champs
Mouzay
Forêt de Wœvre
Jametz
Longuyon
Pierrepont
Dudelange
Rumelange
Crusnes
Aumetz
Boult-aux-Bois
Buzancy
Nouart
Dun-sur-Meuse
Bantheville
Grandpré
Damvillers
Mangiennes
Spincourt
Audun-le-Roman
Algrange
Hayange
Landres
Piennes
Trieux
Nilvange
Florange
Thionville
Yutz
Cattenom
Sierck-les-Bains
Halstroff
Rehlingen-Siersburg
Metzervisse
Dalstein
Bouzonville
Montfaucon-d'Argonne
Malancourt
Sivry-sur-Meuse
Bouligny
Plaine de la Wœvre
Avril
Fameck
Rombas
Jœuf
Briey
Guénange
Hagondange
Freistroff
Cernay-en-Dormois
ARGONNE
Varennes-en-Argonne
Montzéville
Étain
Fléville-Lixières
Homécourt
Auboué
Ville-sur-Tourbe
Belleville-sur-Meuse
Neuvilly-en-Argonne
Warcq
Verdun
Conflans-en-Jarnisy
Jarny
Woippy
Metz
Vigy
Noisseville
Boulay-Moselle
Creutzwald
La Neuville-au-Pont
Ste-Menehould
Clermont-en-Argonne
Futeau
Dugny-sur-Meuse
Dieue-sur-Meuse
Manheulles
Fresnes-en-Woëvre
Gravelotte
Ars-sur-Moselle
Montigny-lès-Metz
Marly
Courcelles-Chaussy
Faulquemont
Chambley-Bussières
Gorze
Auve
Villers-en-Argonne
Seuil-d'Argonne
Souilly
Les Éparges
Jouy-aux-Arches
Pagny-sur-Moselle
Verny
Han-sur-Nied
Dommartin-Varimont
Givry-en-Argonne
Beausite
Vaubecourt
Troyon
Vigneulles-lès-Hattonchâtel
LORRAINE
Luppy
Baronville
Possesse
Laheycourt
Rembercourt-Sommaisne
Chaumont-sur-Aire
Pierrefitte-sur-Aire
Dompcevrin
Thiaucourt-Regniéville
Heudicourt-sous-les-Côtes
Pont-à-Mousson
Plateau Lorrain
Nomeny
Delme
Nettancourt
Laimont
St-Mihiel
Apremont-la-Forêt
Flirey
Revigny-sur-Ornain
Heiltz-le-Maurupt
Villotte-sur-Aire
Sampigny
Rambucourt
Dieulouard
Aulnois-sur-Seille
Château-Salins
Fains-Véel
Naives-Rosières
Bar-le-Duc
Lérouville
Commercy
Euville
Ménil-la-Tour
Domèvre-en-Haye
Custines
Brin-sur-Seille
SAULNOIS
Pargny-sur-Saulx
Robert-Espagne
Longeville-en-Barrois
Tronville-en-Barrois
Sorcy-St-Martin
Lucey
Pompey
Frouard
Bouxières-aux-Dames
Moncel-sur-Seille
Vic-sur-Seille
Cheminon
Villiers-en-Lieu
Brillon-en-Barrois
Ligny-en-Barrois
Void-Vacon
Foug
Toul
Gondreville
Nancy
St-Max
Laxou
Jarville-la-Malgrange
Einville-au-Jard
St-Dizier
Stainville
Ancerville
Écrouves
Villers-lès-Nancy
Chaligny
St-Nicolas-de-Port
Lunéville
Eurville-Bienville
Cousances-les-Forges
Morley
Domgermain
Vaucouleurs
Treveray
Demange-aux-Eaux
Houdelaincourt
Blénod-lès-Toul
Vitrerie
Richardménil
Flavigny-sur-Moselle
Damelevières
Éclaron-Braucourt-Ste-Livière
Rachecourt-sur-Marne
Chevillon
Montiers-sur-Saulx
Gondrecourt-le-Château
Colombey-les-Belles
Crépey
Ceintrey
Crévéchamps
St-Clément
Voillecomte
Wassy
Brousseval
Thonnance-lès-Joinville
Mandres-en-Barrois
Autreville
Vézelise
Tantonville
Haroué
Bayon
Montier-en-Der
Dommartin-le-Franc
Joinville
Poissons
Domrémy-la-Pucelle
Greux
Dainville-Bertheléville
Martigny-les-Gerbonvaux
XAINTOIS
Vaudémont
Gerbamont
St-Firmin
Charmes
Louze
Sommevoire
Germay
Coussey
Ménil-sur-Belvitte
BARROIS
VALLAGE
Moselle
Meuse
Marne
Sûre
Saar
Chiers
Aire
Aisne
Semois
Ourthe
Our
Prüm
Lesse

Saarbrücken
Kaiserslautern
Mannheim
Ludwigshafen am Rhein
Heidelberg
Karlsruhe
Strasbourg
Wiesbaden
Mainz
Worms
Pirmasens
Zweibrücken
Homburg
Neunkirchen
St Wendel
Idar-Oberstein
Bad Kreuznach
Bingen am Rhein
Rüsselsheim
Neustadt an der Weinstraße
Landau in der Pfalz
Speyer
Baden-Baden
Rastatt
Offenburg
Haguenau
Saverne
Sarrebourg
Sarreguemines
Bitche
Wissembourg
Völklingen
Forbach
Bernkastel-Kues
Cochem
Boppard
Alzey
Frankenthal
Bad Dürkheim
Germersheim
Bruchsal
Ettlingen
Pforzheim
Freudenstadt
Obernai
Molsheim
Schiltigheim
Kehl
Bühl
Achern
Wittlich
Morbach
Hermeskeil
Tholey
Lebach
St Ingbert
Blieskastel
Landstuhl
Kusel
Rockenhausen
Grünstadt
Eisenberg
Kirn
Simmern
Kastellaun
Gemünden
Monzingen
Meisenheim
Lauterbourg
Wörth am Rhein
Kandel
Bad Bergzabern
Dahn
Rodalben
Waldfischbach-Burgalben
NORDPFÄLZER BERGLAND
Hunsrück
Soonwald
Idarwald
Pfälzer Wald
Eifel
Vosges
Taunus
Bensheim
Lampertheim
Viernheim
Walldorf
Wiesloch
Hockenheim
Sandhausen
Waghäusel
Schwetzingen
Oppenheim
Nierstein
Groß-Gerau
Langen
Darmstadt
Griesheim
Pfungstadt
Hofheim am Taunus
Eltville am Rhein
Bad Schwalbach
Ingelheim am Rhein
Gensingen
Nahe
Rhein (Rhine)
Mosel
Saar
D
A
B
C
4
5
6
29

1
2
3
A
B
C
D
Cork, Rosslare
Plymouth
Pte du Château
Plougrescant
Perros-Guirec
Penvénan
Trégastel
Louannec
Plouguiel
Pleumeur-Bodou
Tréguier
Trébeurden
Lannion
La Roche-Derrien
TRÉGORROI
Pontrieux
Île de Batz
Roscoff
Baie de Morlaix
Pte de Primel
Baie de Lannion
Plougasnou
Locquirec
St-Pol-de-Léon
Ploubezre
Brignogan-Plage
Plouescat
Cléder
Carantec
Lanmeur
Ploumilliau
Plestin-les-Grèves
Pluzunet
Plouaret
Bégard
Kerlouan
Guissény
Taulé
St-Martin-des-Champs
Menez Bré
Plouguerneau
Plouzévédé
PAYS DE LÉON
Lannilis
Plouvorn
Morlaix
Plounévez-Moëdec
Grâces
Guingamp
Ploudalmézeau
Plouguin
Lesneven
Le Folgoët
Plouigneau
Plougonven
Belle-Isle-en-Terre
Ploumagoar
Porspoder
Landivisiau
St-Thégonnec
Pleyber-Christ
Moustéru
Brélès
Plabennec
Lampaul-Plouarzel
Milizac
Gouesnou
Landerneau
Lampaul-Guimiliau
Plougonver
Bourbriac
Plouarzel
St-Renan
Bohars
Guipavas
Ploudiry
St-Sauveur
Plouzané
Guilers
Le Relecq-Kerhuon
Sizun
Roc'h Trévezel
Berrien
Callac
Locmaria-Plouzané
Brest
Le Conquet
Goulet de Brest
Plougastel-Daoulas
Daoulas
Huelgoat
Pte de St-Mathieu
Monts d'Arrée
Montagne St-Michel
Poullaouen
St-Nicolas-du-Pélem
Roscanvel
Hanvec
Plouyé
Camaret-sur-Mer
Le Faou
Carhaix-Plouguer
Maël-Carhaix
Pte de Penhir
Presqu'île de Crozon
Pont-de-Buis-lès-Quimerch
Plonévez-du-Faou
Plounévez-Quintin
Mer d'Iroise
Morgat
Crozon
Menez Hom
Pleyben
Landeleau
Rostrenen
Plouguernével
Gouarec
Cap de la Chèvre
Baie de Douarnenez
Plomodiern
Châteaulin
Châteauneuf-du-Faou
Roc de Toullaëron
Montagnes Noires
Mûr-de-
Plouray
Gourin
Silfiac
Plonévez-Porzay
Locronan
Briec
Douarnenez
Séglien
Île de Sein
Le Cap
Plogonnec
CORNOUAILLE
Coray
Guémené-sur-Scorff
Pte du Raz
Audierne
Pont-Croix
Plouhinec
Quimper
Torch
Scaër
Le Faouët
Landudec
Ergué-Gabéric
Kernascléden
Plozévet
Pouldreuzic
St-Yvy
Rosporden
St-Thurien
Inguiniel
Bubry
Baie d'Audierne
Bannalec
Tréméven
Mellac
Plouay
Plonéour-Lanvern
Pleuven
Fouesnant
Melgven
Quimperlé
Pont-l'Abbé
Bénodet
Concarneau
Inzinzac-Lochrist
Plomeur
Anse de Bénodet
Trégunc
Riec-sur-Bélon
Pont-Aven
St-Guénolé
Loctudy
Névez
Moëlan-sur-Mer
Guidel
Caudan
Hennebont
Penmarch
Plobannalec
Clohars-Carnoët
Pte de Penmarch
Guilvinec
Lesconil
Le Pouldu
Lanester
Anse de Pouldu
Lorient
Ploemeur
Merlevenez
Riantec
Larmor-Plage
Port-Louis
Plouhinec
Belz
Île de Groix
Groix
Erdeven
Plouharnel
Presqu'île de Quiberon
St-Pierre-Quiberon
Quiberon
Sauzon
Belle-Île
E50
E60
N12
N164
N165
D786
D767
D887
D789
D785
D783
D765

4
5
6
16
24
A
B
C
D
Channel Islands
Portsmouth
Golfe de St-Malo
Île de Bréhat
Pte de l'Arcouest
Îles Chausey
Coutances
Cerisy-la-Salle
Montmartin-sur-Mer
Quettreville-sur-Sienne
Hambye
Percy
Bréhal
Cérences
Gavray
Villedieu-les-Poêles
St-Sever-Calvados
Donville-les-Bains
Granville
St-Pair-sur-Mer
La Haye-Pesnel
Jullouville
Sartilly
Carolles
St-Pois
Brécey
Pte du Grouin
Cancale
Baie du Mont-St-Michel
Genêts
Avranches
Pontaubault
Ducey
Cap Fréhel
Rothéneuf
Paramé
St-Méloir-des-Ondes
Le-Vivier-sur-Mer
Dinard
St-Malo
St-Lunaire
St-Briac-sur-Mer
Sables-d'Or-les-Pins
Fréhel
Erquy
Pléneuf-Val-André
Étables-sur-Mer
Binic
Baie de St-Brieuc
Matignon
St-Jouan-des-Guérets
Ploubalay
Châteauneuf-d'Ille-et-Vilaine
Pontorson
Dol-de-Bretagne
Pleine-Fougères
St-James
St-Martin-de-Landelles
Argouges
Louvigné-du-Désert
Plérin
St-Brieuc
Langueux
Ploufragan
Trégueux
Châtelaudren
Plélo
St-Alban
Hénanbihen
Plancoët
Lamballe
Corseul
Pleudihen-sur-Rance
Miniac-Morvan
Trans
Antrain
St-Brice-en-Coglès
Dinan
St-Pierre-de-Plesguen
Cuguen
Maroué
Quessoy
Plaintel
PENTHIÈVRE
Jugon-les-Lacs
Léhon
Meillac
Combourg
Dingé
Romazy
Lécousse
Fougères
Moncontour
Plénée-Jugon
Yvignac
Évran
Tinténiac
Sens-de-Bretagne
Romagné
La Pellerine
Plœuc-sur-Lié
Landes du Mené
Bel Air
Collinée
Broons
Éréac
Caulnes
Bécherel
Hédé
St-Aubin-d'Aubigné
Gosné
St-Aubin-du-Cormier
St-Pierre-des-Landes
Uzel
Plouguenast
Irodouër
Romillé
Gévezé
Liffré
La Bouëxière
La Croixille
Trévé
Loudéac
Plémet
Merdrignac
Montauban-de-Bretagne
St-Méen-le-Grand
La Chapelle-des-Fougeretz
Betton
Val-d'Izé
Bédée
Breteil
Boisgervilly
Cesson-Sévigné
Servon-sur-Vilaine
Vitré
Châteaubourg
Ménéac
La Chèze
La Trinité-Porhoët
Iffendic
Talensac
Montfort
Rennes
Noyal-Pontivy
Rohan
Bréhan
Mauron
Mordelles
St-Jacques-de-la-Lande
Bruz
Châteaugiron
Argentré-du-Plessis
Guilliers
Forêt de Paimpont
Paimpont
Goven
Vern-sur-Seiche
Bais
Naizin
Josselin
Ploërmel
Plélan-le-Grand
Maxent
Baulon
Corps-Nuds
Janzé
La Guerche-de-Bretagne
Pluméliau
Moréac
Remungol
Guégon
Campénéac
Guichen
Le-Theil-de-Bretagne
Retiers
Locminé
Bignan
Guer
Guignen
Maure-de-Bretagne
Lohéac
Le Sel-de-Bretagne
La Roë
St-Jean-Brévelay
Plumelec
Sérent
Ruffiac
Carentoir
Pipriac
Guipry
Messac
Bain-de-Bretagne
Martigné-Ferchaud
Congrier
Landes de Lanvaux
Malestroit
Teillay
Rougé
Grand-Champ
Plumergat
Monterblanc
Elven
La Gacilly
Grand-Fougeray
Soudan
Châteaubriant
Brech
Plescop
St-Avé
Rochefort-en-Terre
Peillac
Malansac
Derval
Erbray
St-Julien-de-Vouvantes
Pluneret
Auray
Ploeren
Vannes
Sulniac
Questembert
Theix
Redon
St-Nicolas-de-Redon
Allaire
Guémené-Penfao
Moisdon-la-Rivière
Arradon
Baden
Noyalo
Noyal-Muzillac
Rieux
Fégréac
Marsac-sur-Don
Nozay
La Meilleraye-de-Bretagne
Surzur
Ambon
Muzillac
Péaule
Marzan
St-Dolay
Plessé
Saffré
St-Mars-la-Jaille
Sarzeau
St-Gildas-de-Rhuys
Presqu'île de Rhuys
La Roche-Bernard
Nivillac
Guenrouet
Blain
Riaillé
Damgan
Pénestin
Missillac
St-Gildas-des-Bois
Joué-sur-Erdre
Férel
Herbignac
Pontchâteau
Nort-sur-Erdre
Mésanger
Assérac
Campbon
Fay-de-Bretagne
Héric
Ligné
Ancenis
Île d'Houat
Île de Hœdic
GRANDE BRIÈRE
Mesquer
Piriac-sur-Mer
St-Joachim
Montoir-de-Bretagne
Bouvron
Petit-Mars
St-Mars-du-Désert
Oudon
Savenay
Guérande
La Turballe
Donges
Cordemais
La Chapelle-sur-Erdre
Carquefou
Liré
Champtoceaux
La Baule-Escoublac
Le Croisic
Batz-sur-Mer
Pte de Croisic
Le Pouliguen
Pornichet
Trignac
St-Nazaire
Loire
Paimbœuf
St-Étienne-de-Montluc
Sautron
Orvault
Thouaré-sur-Loire
St-Laurent-des-Autels
Le Fuilet
St-Julien-de-Concelles
St-Brevin-les-Pins
St-Père-en-Retz
Couëron
St-Herblain
Nantes
Rezé
Basse-Goulaine
St-Sébastien-sur-Loire
Gesté
St-Michel-Chef-Chef
Rouans
Le Pellerin
Bouguenais
Vertou
Vallet
Vilaine
Rance
Ille
Seiche
Chère
Oust
Canal de Nantes à Brest
E50
E401
E03
E60
E03/401
A84
N12
N24
N137
N164
N165
N166
N171
N175
N176

Dinard
St-Malo
Mont-St-Michel
Pontaubault
Ducey
Mortain
St-Hilaire-du-Harcouët
Barenton
Lamballe
Plancoët
Dol-de-Bretagne
Dinan
Combourg
Antrain
Fougères
Lécousse
Jugon-les-Lacs
Évran
Tinténiac
Broons
Caulnes
Bécherel
Hédé
St-Aubin-d'Aubigné
Liffré
St-Aubin-du-Cormier
Ernée
Montaubaudin
Merdrignac
Montauban-de-Bretagne
St-Méen-le-Grand
Betton
Cesson-Sévigné
Rennes
Vitré
Laval
Montfort
Mordelles
Mauron
Paimpont
Plélan-le-Grand
Ploërmel
Bruz
Janzé
La Guerche-de-Bretagne
Bain-de-Bretagne
Guer
Malestroit
Craon
Château-Gontier
Châteaubriant
Pouancé
Segré
Redon
St-Nicolas-de-Redon
Derval
Nozay
Blain
La Roche-Bernard
Pontchâteau
Candé
Ancenis
Guérande
La Baule-Escoublac
St-Nazaire
Savenay
Nantes
Rezé
St-Sébastien-sur-Loire
Carquefou
Orvault
La Chapelle-sur-Erdre
Couëron
Bouguenais
Vertou
Clisson
Cholet
Pornic
Machecoul
Noirmoutier-en-l'Île
Île de Noirmoutier
Baie de Bourgneuf
Challans
St-Jean-de-Monts
Les Herbiers
Montaigu
Mortagne-sur-Sèvre
Rocheservière
Legé
GRANDE BRIÈRE
PAYS DE RETZ
SEGRÉEN
LES MAUGES
Loire
Vilaine
Rance
Forêt de Paimpont
E50
E60
E03
E62
A11
A81
A83
A84
A87
E401
N12
N24
N137
N157
N165
N171
N176
16
23
30
1
2
3
A
B
C
D

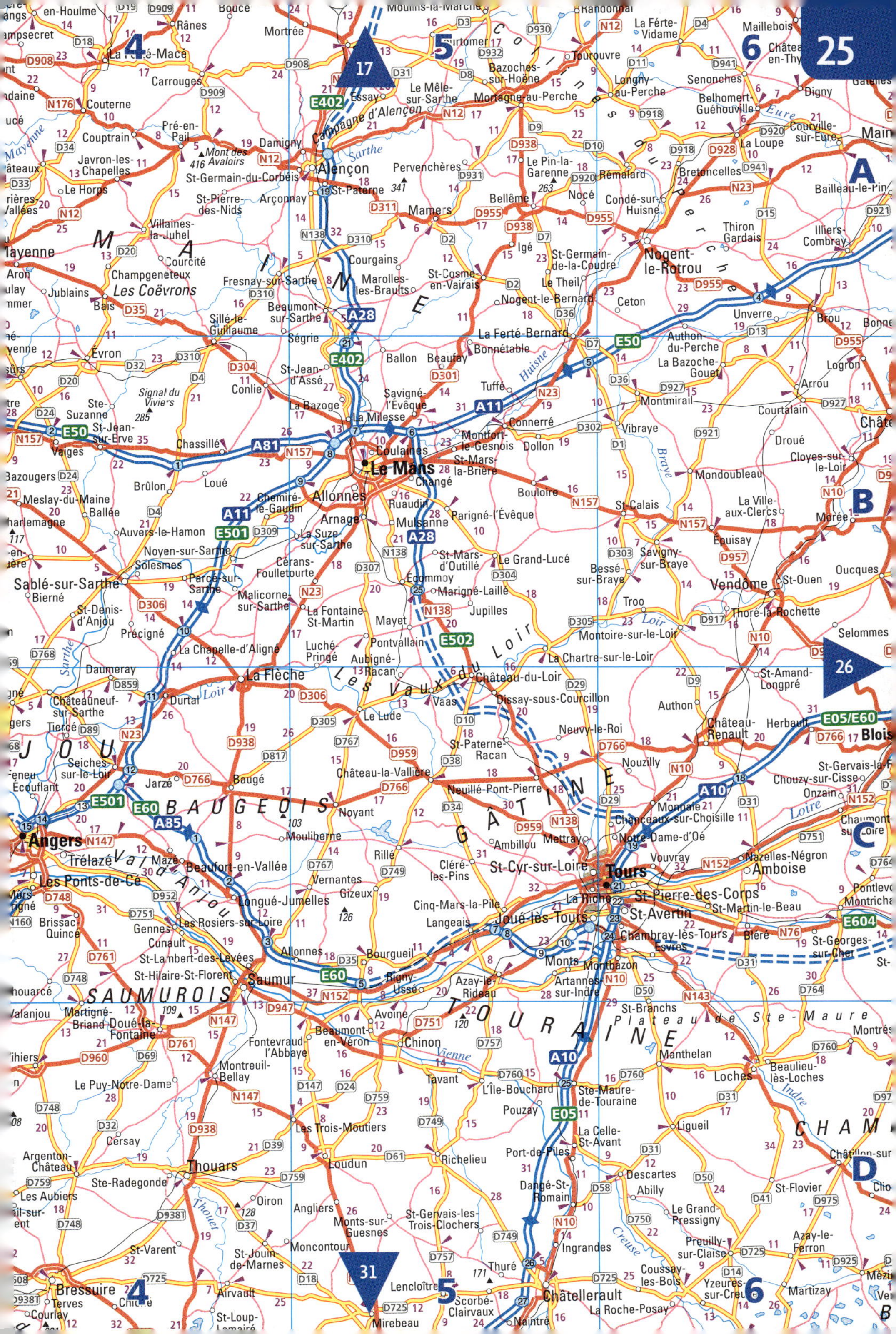

17
26
31
4
5
6
A
B
C
D
Alençon
Mamers
Mortagne-au-Perche
Bellême
Nogent-le-Rotrou
La Ferté-Bernard
Le Mans
Sablé-sur-Sarthe
La Flèche
Angers
Saumur
Chinon
Tours
Amboise
Blois
Vendôme
Château-du-Loir
Château-Renault
Loches
Châtellerault
Loudun
Thouars
Bressuire
Mirebeau
Lencloître
Richelieu
Doué-la-Fontaine
Montreuil-Bellay
Baugé
Le Lude
Château-la-Vallière
Neuillé-Pont-Pierre
Joué-lès-Tours
St-Pierre-des-Corps
St-Avertin
Chambray-lès-Tours
St-Cyr-sur-Loire
La Riche
Montbazon
Azay-le-Rideau
Langeais
Bourgueil
Longué-Jumelles
Beaufort-en-Vallée
Les Ponts-de-Cé
Trélazé
Durtal
Châteauneuf-sur-Sarthe
Sillé-le-Guillaume
Beaumont-sur-Sarthe
Mayenne
Évron
Villaines-la-Juhel
Pré-en-Pail
La Ferté-Macé
Carrouges
Couterne
Bonnétable
Montmirail
St-Calais
Bouloire
Ecommoy
Mulsanne
Allonnes
Coulaines
Changé
Arnage
Montoire-sur-le-Loir
La Chartre-sur-le-Loir
Mondoubleau
Brou
La Loupe
Senonches
Châteauneuf-en-Thymerais
Illiers-Combray
Bailleau-le-Pin
Courville-sur-Eure
Rémalard
Longny-au-Perche
Tourouvre
Le Mêle-sur-Sarthe
Essay
St-Paterne
Sainte-Maure-de-Touraine
La Celle-St-Avant
Port-de-Piles
Dangé-St-Romain
Descartes
Ligueil
Preuilly-sur-Claise
La Roche-Posay
Yzeures-sur-Creuse
Le Grand-Pressigny
Châtillon-sur-Indre
Bléré
Montrichard
Vouvray
Monnaie
Nazelles-Négron
Pontlevoy
Herbault
Onzain
Chaumont-sur-Loire
Chouzy-sur-Cisse
St-Gervais-la-Forêt
Selommes
St-Amand-Longpré
Morée
Cloyes-sur-le-Loir
Droué
Courtalain
Vibraye
Dollon
Connerré
Savigné-l'Évêque
Ballon
Beaufay
Tuffé
Marolles-les-Braults
Fresnay-sur-Sarthe
Bais
Jublains
Le Horps
Javron-les-Chapelles
Couptrain
St-Pierre-des-Nids
Arçonnay
Loué
Brûlon
Chassillé
Vaiges
Meslay-du-Maine
Ballée
Noyen-sur-Sarthe
Parcé-sur-Sarthe
Malicorne-sur-Sarthe
Cérans-Foulletourte
La Suze-sur-Sarthe
Parigné-l'Évêque
Le Grand-Lucé
Bessé-sur-Braye
Mayet
Pontvallain
Jupilles
Dissay-sous-Courcillon
Neuvy-le-Roi
Nouzilly
Noyant
Rillé
Gizeux
Vernantes
Mouliherne
Jarzé
Seiches-sur-le-Loir
Tiercé
Brissac-Quincé
Gennes
Les Rosiers-sur-Loire
Allonnes
Fontevraud-l'Abbaye
Avoine
Beaumont-en-Véron
L'Île-Bouchard
Richelieu
Les Trois-Moutiers
Moncontour
Airvault
St-Varent
Argenton-Château
Ste-Radegonde
Oiron
Le Puy-Notre-Dame
Vihiers
Cersay
Mettray
Ambillou
Cinq-Mars-la-Pile
Cléré-les-Pins
Manthelan
Beaulieu-lès-Loches
Esvres
Artannes-sur-Indre
Monts
Ste-Maure-de-Touraine
Pouzay
Tavant
Ingrandes
Naintré
Scorbé-Clairvaux
Thuré
Coussay-les-Bois
Azay-le-Ferron
Martizay
Abilly
MAINE
BAUGEOIS
SAUMUROIS
GÂTINE
TOURAINE
Collines du Perche
Les Coëvrons
Les Vaux du Loir
Val d'Anjou
Plateau de Ste-Maure
Mayenne
Sarthe
Loir
Loire
Vienne
Indre
Creuse
Huisne
Braye
Thouet
Eure
A10
A11
A28
A81
A85
E05
E50
E60
E402
E501
E502
E604
E05/E60
N10
N12
N23
N138
N143
N147
N152
N157
N176
N76

Rambouillet
Forêt de Rambouillet
St-Arnoult-en-Yvelines
HUREPOIX
18
Évry
Corbeil-Essonnes
Arpajon
Mennecy
Melun
Cesson
Vaux-le-Pénil
Guignes
Mormant
Tréon
Tremblay-les-Villages
Nogent-le-Roi
Épernon
Maintenon
Pierres
Thimert-Gâtelles
Digny
Gallardon
Jouy
Courville-sur-Eure
La Loupe
Mainvilliers
Lèves
Lucé
Chartres
Luisant
Auneau
Ablis
Dourdan
Étréchy
La Ferté-Alais
Milly-la-Forêt
Perthes
Fontainebleau
Champagne-sur-Seine
Avon
Forêt de Fontainebleau
Bourron-Marlotte
Moret-sur-Loing
Béville-le-Comte
Étampes
Maisse
Bailleau-le-Pin
Thivars
Sours
Sainville
Dammarie
Ouarville
Illiers-Combray
Méréville
Angerville
Sermaises
Malesherbes
La Chapelle-la-Reine
St-Pierre-lès-Nemours
Nemours
Bagneaux-sur-Loing
Larchant
Le Gault-St-Denis
Voves
Ymonville
Unverre
Brou
Bonneval
Sancheville
B E A U C E
Janville
Toury
Outarville
Pithiviers
Puiseaux
Souppes-sur-Loing
Château-Landon
Dordives
Orgères-en-Beauce
Loigny-la-Bataille
Logron
Arrou
Courtalain
Châteaudun
Droué
Terminiers
Aschères-le-Marché
Bazoches-les-Gallerandes
GÂTINAIS
Boynes
Corbeilles
Ferrières
Neuville-aux-Bois
Artenay
Patay
Chilleurs-aux-Bois
Beaune-la-Rolande
Boiscommun
Pannes
Châlette-sur-Loing
Cloyes-sur-le-Loir
La Ferté-Villeneuil
O R L É A N A I S
Chevilly
Loury
Traînou
Ladon
Bellegarde
Villemandeur
Montargis
Amilly
Épieds-en-Beauce
Ouzouer-le-Marché
Saran
Fleury-les-Aubrais
Vimory
Coulmiers
St-Jean-de-la-Ruelle
Orléans
St-Jean-de-Braye
Chécy
Châteauneuf-sur-Loire
Lorris
Morée
Binas
Jargeau
Sandillon
Meung-sur-Loire
St-Ay
Olivet
Marchenoir
Oucques
St-Ouen
Josnes
Beaugency
Cléry-St-André
St-Benoît-sur-Loire
Nogent-sur-Vernisson
Les Bordes
Sully-sur-Loire
Ouzouer-sur-Loire
Marcilly-en-Villette
Tigy
Lailly-en-Val
Jouy-le-Potier
Selommes
Mer
St-Laurent-Nouan
La Ferté-St-Aubin
Val d'Orléans
La Bussière
Gien
25
Suèvres
Ménars
La Chaussée-St-Victor
Herbault
Blois
La Ferté-St-Cyr
Isdes
Vouzon
Cerdon
Coullons
Briare
Chambord
Vineuil
St-Gervais-la-Forêt
Lamotte-Beuvron
Brinon-sur-Sauldre
Châtillon-sur-Loire
S O L O G N E
Chouzy-sur-Cisse
Onzain
Cellettes
Bracieux
Neung-sur-Beuvron
Nouan-le-Fuzelier
Argent-sur-Sauldre
Blancafort
Beaulieu-sur-Loire
Bonny
Cour-Cheverny
Chaumont-sur-Loire
Aubigny-sur-Nère
Oizon
Vailly-sur-Sauldre
Léré
Amboise
Contres
Soings-en-Sologne
Marcilly-en-Gault
Souesmes
Savigny-en-Sancerre
Pontlevoy
Montrichard
Mur-de-Sologne
Selles-St-Denis
Salbris
Bannay
Chémery
Pruniers-en-Sologne
Romorantin-Lanthenay
La Ferté-Imbault
Nançay
La Chapelle-d'Angillon
Collines du Sancerrois
Sancerre
St-Georges-sur-Cher
St-Romain-sur-Cher
Villefranche-sur-Cher
Theillay
Neuvy-sur-Barangeon
Henrichemont
St-Aignan
Noyers-sur-Cher
Selles-sur-Cher
Gièvres
Mennetou-sur-Cher
Vierzon
Chabris
St-Christophe-en-Bazelle
Allogny
Menetou-Salon
Mesves-sur-Loire
Montrésor
Valençay
Genouilly
Méreau
Foëcy
Mehun-sur-Yèvre
St-Martin-d'Auxigny
Les Aix-d'Angillon
Sancergues
Nouans-les-Fontaines
Poulaines
Massay
Graçay
Fussy
Écueillé
Luçay-le-Mâle
Lury-sur-Arnon
Marmagne
St-Doulchard
St-Germain-du-Puy
Baugy
Vatan
Bourges
CHAMPAGNE BERRICHONNE
La Chapelle-St-Ursin
Trouy
Avord
Nérondes
Châtillon-sur-Indre
Pellevoisin
Palluau-sur-Indre
Levroux
Ste-Lizaigne
Chârost
St-Florent-sur-Cher
Clion
Issoudun
Civray
St-Genou
Vineuil
Lunery
Levet
La Guerche-sur-l'Aubois
Azay-le-Ferron
Buzançais
Dun-sur-Auron
Blet
Villedieu-sur-Indre
Neuvy-Pailloux
Chalivoy-Milon
Thaumiers
Mézières-en-Brenne
Niherne
Déols
St-Maur
Châteauroux
Martizay
Vendœuvres
Ambrault
Meillant
B E R R Y
B R E N N E
32
Loire
Cher
Indre
Eure
Essonne
Canal d'Orléans
Canal de Briare
Canal du Berry
Auron
434
221

19
28
33
4
5
6
A
B
C
D
Provins
Nogent-sur-Seine
Romilly-sur-Seine
Sens
Troyes
La Chapelle-St-Luc
Pont-Ste-Marie
Ste-Savine
St-André-les-Vergers
Villeneuve-l'Archevêque
Aix-en-Othe
Joigny
Migennes
Auxerre
St-Florentin
Tonnerre
Chablis
Avallon
Vézelay
Clamecy
Montbard
Semur-en-Auxois
Vitteaux
Saulieu
Châtillon-sur-Seine
Bar-sur-Seine
Bar-sur-Aube
Brienne-le-Château
Arcis-sur-Aube
Pouilly-en-Auxois
Arnay-le-Duc
Beaune
Nevers
Decize
Autun
Le Creusot
Château-Chinon
Varzy
Corbigny
Luzy
Nolay
La Charité-sur-Loire
CHAMPAGNE
CHAMPAGNE HUMIDE
CHAMPAGNE
CÔTE DES BARS
PAYS D'OTHE
Forêt d'Othe
CHÂTILLONNAIS
AUXERROIS
Terre Plaine
Morvan
AUTUNOIS
AUXOIS
CÔTE D'OR
Puisaye
Val de Seine
Montois
Lac du Der Étang de la Horre
Lac du Temple
Lac des Settons
A5
A6
A19
A26
A38
A77
E15/60
E17/54
E54
E54/511
E511
E15
N6
N7
N19
N60
N71
N77
N80
N81
N151
Seine
Aube
Yonne
Armançon
Cure
Ource
Canal de la Haute Seine
Canal du Nivernais
Mont Tasselot 598
Mont Aigue 605
Haut-Folin 901
Le Télégraphe 800
Mont Julien 681

St-Dizier
Stainville
Ancerville
Eurville-Bienville
Cousances-les-Forges
Morley
Treveray
Demange-aux-Eaux
Vaucouleurs
Houdelaincourt
Gondrecourt-le-Château
Domgermain
Écrouves
Villers-lès-Nancy
Laxou
Jarville-la-Malgrange
Einville-au-Jard
St-Nicolas-de-Port
Lunéville
Chaligny
Richardménil
Flavigny-sur-Moselle
Dameleivières
St-Clément
Crévéchamps
Bayon
Tantonville
Haroué
Ceintrey
Vézelise
Crépey
Colombey-les-Belles
Autreville
Blénod-lès-Toul
Vitrey
Rachecourt-sur-Marne
Chevillon
Montiers-sur-Saulx
Voillecomte
Wassy
Brousseval
Montier-en-Der
Dommartin-le-Franc
Joinville
Thonnance-lès-Joinville
Mandres-en-Barrois
Domrémy-la-Pucelle
Greux
Martigny-les-Gerbonvaux
Dainville-Bertheléville
Poissons
Germay
V A L L A G E
X A I N T O I S
Vaudémont
541
St-Firmin
Damas-aux-Bois
Ménil-sur-Belvitte
Charmes
Sommevoire
Blaiserives
Doulaincourt-Saucourt
Neufchâteau
Coussey
Donjeux
Beurville
Cirey-sur-Blaise
Gudmont-Villiers
Roches-Bettaincourt
St-Blin-Semilly
Liffol-le-Grand
Châtenois
Dombasle-en-Xaintois
Poussay
Mirecourt
Mattaincourt
Vincey
Portieux
Nomexy
Châtel-sur-Moselle
Rambervillers
Igney
Padoux
Thaon-les-Vosges
Chavelot
Hymont
Houécourt
Arrentières
Bar-sur-Aube
Colombey-les-Deux-Églises
Vignory
Andelot-Blancheville
Prez-sous-Lafauche
P l a i n e   L o r r a i n e
Bulgnéville
Valfroicourt
Bologne
Bayel
St-Thiébault
Bourmont
Vittel
Contrexéville
Darnieulles
Golbey
Épinal
Girancourt
Les Forges
Juzennecourt
Maranville
Villiers-le-Sec
Chaumont
Millières
Vrécourt
Martigny-les-Bains
F
Jarménil
Uriménil
Pouxeux
Aube
Pont-la-Ville
Bricon
Brottes
Biesles
Clefmont
Breuvannes-en-Bassigny
Darney
Hennezel
Hadol
Xertigny
Châteauvillain
Semoutiers-Montsaon
Foulain
Nogent
Is-en-Bassigny
Meuse
Merrey
Lamarche
Mont des Fourches
500
Monthureux-sur-Saône
Canal de l'Est
Gruey-lès-Surance
La Chapelle-aux-Bois
Bains-les-Bains
Remiremont
Val-de-Meuse
B A S S I G N Y
Serqueux
Isches
Fresnes-sur-Apance
La Vôge
Fontenoy-le-Château
Plombières-les-Bains
Rupt-sur-Moselle
Arc-en-Barrois
Rolampont
Marac
Langres
Neuilly-l'Évêque
Bourbonne-les-Bains
Andilly-en-Bassigny
Corre
Vauvillers
Aillevillers-et-Lyaumont
St-Loup-sur-Semouse
Fougerolles
La Chaume
Rochetaillée
Haute-Amance
Chaudenay
Laferté-sur-Amance
Melay
Polaincourt-et-Clairefontaine
Fontaine-lès-Luxeuil
Luxeuil-les-Bains
Froideconche
Voulaines-les-Templiers
Leuglay
Perrogney-les-Fontaines
Sts-Geosmes
Chalindrey
Jussey
Conflans-sur-Lanterne
Amance
Breuches
St-Sauveur
Auberive
Le Vallinot-Longeau-Percey
Fayl-la-Forêt
Vitrey-sur-Mance
Arbecey
Faverney
La Villedieu-en-Fontenette
Grancey-le-Château-Nouvelle
Aignay-le-Duc
Minot
Étalante
Chassigny-Aisey
Prauthoy
Grenant
Cintrey
P l a t e a u   d e   H a u t e - S a ô n e
Combeaufontaine
Port-sur-Saône
Saulx
Lure
Vy-lès-Lure
Marey-sur-Tille
525
Selongey
Sacquenay
Vauconcourt-Nervezain
Scey-sur-Saône-et-St-Albin
Vaivre-et-Montoille
Vesoul
Noroy-le-Bourg
Gouhenans
Champlitte
Noidans-lès-Vesoul
Échenoz-la-Méline
Villersexel
Montigny-Mornay-Villeneuve-sur-Vingeanne
Membrey
Soing
Lamargelle
Moloy
Is-sur-Tille
Fontaine-Française
Dampierre-sur-Salon
Beaujeu-St-Vallier-Pierrejux-et-Quitteur
Fresne-St-Mamès
Grandvelle-et-le-Perrenot
Dampierre-sur-Linotte
Esprels
Courchaton
Villecomte
Saussy
Til-Châtel
Gemeaux
Lux
Autrey-lès-Gray
Arc-lès-Gray
Gray
Chargey-lès-Gray
La Chapelle-St-Quillain
Fretigney-et-Velloreille
Montbozon
Rougemont
L'Isle-sur-le-Doubs
531
St-Seine-l'Abbaye
Bèze
Mantoche
Gy
Bucey-lès-Gy
Oiselay-et-Grachaux
Rioz
Loulans
Avilley
Soye
Val-Suzon
Fontaine-lès-Dijon
Ruffey-lès-Echirey
Mirebeau
Choye
Charcenne
Étuz
Marchaux
Clerval
Mont Aigue
605
Talant
Dijon
St-Apollinaire
Arc-sur-Tille
Talmay
Pontailler-sur-Saône
Bonboillon
Baume-les-Dames
Vellevans
Chenôve
Marsannay-la-Côte
Vonges
Pesmes
Marnay
Miserey-Salines
Novillars
Roulans
Pont-les-Moulins
Sancey-le-Grand
Lamarche-sur-Saône
Vielverge
Montagney
Gevrey-Chambertin
Fénay
Genlis
Montmirey-le-Château
Ougney
Audeux
Franois
Besançon
Aïssey
Laviron
Auxonne
Moissey
Massif de la Serre
Gendrey
Saône
Mamirolle
Gonsans
Pierrefontaine-les-Varans
Vougeot
636
Nuits-St-Georges
Corcelles-lès-Cîteaux
Longecourt-en-Plaine
Les Maillys
Rochefort-sur-Nenon
Dampierre
St-Vit
Boussières
Vercel-Villedieu-le-Camp
Valdahon
Orchamps-Vennes
Comblanchien
Brazey-en-Plaine
Dole
Forêt de Chaux
Quingey
Chenecey-Buillon
Avoudrey
Savigny-lès-Beaune
Broin
St-Jean-de-Losne
Arc-et-Senans
Ornans
Nods
Les Fins
Beaune
St-Aubin
Tavaux
La Loye
Montbarrey
Myon
Amancey
Mouthier-Haute-Pierre
Morteau
Crêt Monniot
1142
Villers
Éternoz
Bolandoz
Montbenoît
Doubs
Labergement-lès-Seurre
Pouilly-sur-Saône
Seurre
Villers-Farlay
Mont Poupet
850
Chaussin
Mont-sous-Vaudrey
Bians-les-Usiers
Demigny
St-Loup-de-la-Salle
Navilly
Chemin
Petit-Noir
Arçon
Chagny
Frontenard
Salins-les-Bains
Levier
Doubs
Le Grand Taureau
1323
Larmont
Pontarlier
Verdun-sur-le-Doubs
Pierre-de-Bresse
Les Essards-Taignevaux
Aumont
Arbois
Forêt de la Joux
Boujailles
Fleurier
Champforgeuil
St-Martin-en-Bresse
St-Bonnet-en-Bresse
Poligny
Cirque du Fer-à-Cheval
Frasne
La Cluse-et-Mijoux
Les Fourgs
Le Chasseron
1607
Étang de Frasne
Lac de St-Point
Chalon-sur-Saône
St-Marcel
St-Germain
Mervans
Commenailles
Sellières
Montrond
Vers-en-Montagne
Mignovillard
Bonnevaux
Malbuisson
Ste-Croix
Grandson
Mont Suchet
Canal de la Marne au Rhin
Marne
Aube
Aujon
Vair
Saône
Ognon
Loue
Amance
20
27
34
A
B
C
D
1
2
3
A5
A31
A33
A36
A38
A39
E17/54
E17/21
E21
E23
E54
E60
E15
E17
A6
N4
N19
N57
N67
N74
N71
N73
N83
N5
N420
N6
D964
D974
D166
D164
D417
D429
D460
D996
D959
D960
D961
D968
D975
D976
D970
D973
D472
D437
D461
D464
D492
D467
D471
D33
D7
D3

Strasbourg
Kehl
Schiltigheim
Lingolsheim
Illkirch-Graffenstaden
Geispolsheim
Bischheim
Mundolsheim
Truchtersheim
Marlenheim
Wasselonne
Dabo
Abreschviller
Lafrimbolle
St-Quirin
Blâmont
Cirey-sur-Vezouze
Domèvre-sur-Vezouze
Badonviller
Pexonne
Allarmont
Mutzig
Rosheim
Obernai
Schirmeck
La Broque
Donon
Bruche
Mousey
Raon-l'Etape
Senones
Moyenmoutier
Col de Saales
Saales
Colroy-la-Grande
Provenchères-sur-Fave
St-Michel-sur-Meurthe
St-Dié
Ste-Marie-aux-Mines
St-Hippolyte
Le Hohwald
Barr
Andlau
St-Blaise-la-Roche
Villé
Scherwiller
Châtenois
Sélestat
Benfeld
Erstein
Rhinau
Taintrux
St-Léonard
Fraize
Col du Bonhomme
Corcieux
Anould
Ribeauvillé
Riquewihr
Kaysersberg
Lapoutroie
Granges-sur-Vologne
Xonrupt-Longemer
Col de la Schlucht
Ingersheim
Wintzenheim
Colmar
Andolsheim
Eguisheim
Munster
Hohneck
Gérardmer
Breisach am Rhein
La Bresse
Cornimont
Rouffach
Le Markstein
Grand Ballon
Guebwiller
Soultz-Haut-Rhin
St-Amarin
Bussang
Col de Bussang
Ballon d'Alsace
Bitschwiller-lès-Thann
Thann
Cernay
Masevaux
Rougemont-le-Château
Giromagny
Polversheim
Wittenheim
Lutterbach
Illzach
Mulhouse
Ensisheim
Fessenheim
Chalampé
Ottmarsheim
Rixheim
Habsheim
Sierentz
Bartenheim
Altkirch
Hirsingue
Dannemarie
Carspach
Fontaine
Offemont
Belfort
Danjoutin
Héricourt
Grandvillars
Delle
Boncourt
Seppois-le-Bas
Ferrette
Audincourt
Hérimoncourt
Alle
Porrentruy
Courgenay
Damvant
Bassecourt
Glère
Doubs
Trévillers
Goumois
Saignelégier
Tramelan
Le Noirmont
Tavannes
Sonceboz
Courtelary
St-Imier
Vallon de St-Imier
Chasseral
Bieler See
Nidau
Biel
Grenchen
Lengnau
Solothurn
Zuchwil
Biberist
Bätterkinden
Büren an der Aare
Fraubrunnen
Kirchberg
Burgdorf
La Chaux-de-Fonds
Dombresson
La Neuveville
Le Locle
Cernier
St-Blaise
Erlach
Ins
Aarberg
Lyss
Urtenen
Münchenbuchsee
Zollikofen
Neuchâtel
Peseux
Boudry
Colombier
Murtensee
Murten
Kerzers
Wohlen
Bolligen
Ostermundigen
BERN
Köniz
Muri
Worb
Belp
Laupen
Estavayer-le-Lac
Avenches
Payerne
Villars-sur-Glâne
Düdingen
Tafers
Fribourg
Schwarzenburg
Riggisberg
Münsingen
Konolfingen
Schlosswil
Signau
Langnau
Eggiwil
Sumiswald
Hasle
Eriswil
Huttwil
Napf
Herzogenbuchsee
Kriegstetten
Wangen
Langenthal
Aarwangen
Niederbipp
Oensingen
Balsthal
Mümliswil
Waldenburg
Delémont
Courrendlin
Moutier
Court
Moron
Hasenmatt
Birse
Laufen
Breitenbach
Zwingen
Reinach
Allschwil
Basel
Pratteln
Liestal
Sissach
Hölstein
Riehen
Weil am Rhein
Lörrach
Rheinfelden
Bad Säckingen
Möhlin
Frick
Laufenburg
Efringen-Kirchen
Binzen
Kandern
Steinen
Schopfheim
Wehr
Görwihl
Rickenbach
Zell im Wiesental
Todtmoos
Schönau im Schwarzwald
Auggen
Schliengen
Badenweiler
Müllheim
Buggingen
Heitersheim
Bad Krozingen
Hartheim
Belchen
Todtnau
Bernau
Feldberg
Hinterzarten
Titisee-Neustadt
Schluchsee
Lenzkirch
Grafenhausen
Häusern
St Blasien
Waldshut
Tiengen
Lauchringen
Albbruck
Dogern
Döttingen
Zurzach
Eglisau
Bülach
Wutöschingen
Eggingen
Stühlingen
Schleitheim
Schaffhausen
Neuhausen
Neunkirch
Lottstetten
Bonndorf im Schwarzwald
Löffingen
Hüfingen
Bräunlingen
Donaueschingen
Bad Dürrheim
Villingen
Schwenningen
Furtwangen im Schwarzwald
St Georgen im Schwarzwald
Königsfeld im Schwarzwald
Hardt
Schramberg
Tennenbronn
Schiltach
Wolfach
Haslach im Kinzigtal
Hausach
Gengenbach
Zell am Harmersbach
Oberharmersbach
Bad Peterstal
Griesbach
Oppenau
Lautenbach
Oberkirch
Renchen
Achern
Sasbach
Ottersweier
Hornisgrinde
Ottenhöfen im Schwarzwald
Baiersbronn
Freudenstadt
Dornstetten
Pfalzgrafenweiler
Waldachtal
Horb am Neckar
Loßburg
Alpirsbach
Sulz am Neckar
Oberndorf am Neckar
Aichhalden
Epfendorf
Rottweil
Offenburg
Ortenberg
Ohlsbach
Durbach
Willstätt
Altenheim
Friesenheim
Lahr
Biberach
Kippenheim
Ettenheim
Herbolzheim
Kenzingen
Malterdingen
Weisweil
Wyhl
Endingen
Teningen
Emmendingen
Elzach
Waldkirch
Kandel
Denzlingen
Gundelfingen
Freiburg im Breisgau
Umkirch
Bötzingen
Reute
Marckolsheim
Oberrotweil
Totenkopf
Vogelgrun
Kirchzarten
Oberried
St Märgen
Breitnau
Neustadt
Aarau
Obergösgen
Olten
Rothrist
Zofingen
Reiden
Murgenthal
Dagmersellen
Sursee
Sempach
Willisau
Menznau
Wolhusen
Werthenstein
Entlebuch
Schüpfheim
Escholzmatt
Flühli
Marbach
Brienzer Rothorn
Hohgant
Lenzburg
Seon
Unterkulm
Reinach
Beinwil
Hallwiler See
Baldegger See
Beromünster
Hochdorf
Eschenbach
Emmen
Neuenkirch
Ruswil
Littau
Luzern
Kriens
Horw
Malters
Hergiswil
Pilatus
Alpnach
Sarnen
Sarner See
Sachseln
Giswil
Kerns
Stans
Buochs
Wolfenschiessen
Engelberg
Uri-Rotstock
Titlis
Vierwaldstätter See
Weggis
Küssnacht
Arth
Ebikon
Zug
Zuger See
Baar
Cham
Sins
Muri
Bremgarten
Wohlen
Brugg
Baden
Wettingen
Neuenhof
Dietikon
Schlieren
Urdorf
Zürich
Wallisellen
Regensdorf
Dielsdorf
Adliswil
Thalwil
Horgen
Wädenswil
HOTZENWALD
SUNDGAU
AJOIE
BREISGAU
MITTELLAND
EMMENTAL
Plaine d'Alsace
Canal du Rhône au Rhin
Rhin (Rhein)
Ill
Aare
Wutach
Lac de Neuchâtel
D
CH
21
35

A
B
C
D
1
2
3
24
36
Barbâtre
Beauvoir-sur-Mer
Fromentine
La Barre-de-Monts
Notre-Dame-de-Monts
St-Gervais
Marais breton
St-Jean-de-Monts
Soullans
Challans
La Garnache
Falleron
Paulx
Legé
Rocheservière
Les Lucs-sur-Boulogne
Palluau
Le Poiré-sur-Vie
Belleville-sur-Vie
Dompierre-sur-Yon
Commequiers
Aizenay
Port-Joinville
Île d'Yeu
St-Hilaire-de-Riez
St-Gilles-Croix-de-Vie
Pte de Grosse Terre
Le Fenouiller
Coëx
Venansault
Jaunay
B O C A G E   V E N D É E N
La Roche-sur-Yon
La Ferrière
La Chaize-le-Vicomte
Brétignolles-sur-Mer
Brem-sur-Mer
La Mothe-Achard
Aubigny
St-Florent-des-Bois
St-Mathurin
Olonne-sur-Mer
Château-d'Olonne
Les Sables-d'Olonne
Pte de l'Aiguille
Talmont-St-Hilaire
Avrillé
Moutiers-les-Mauxfaits
Mareuil-sur-Lay-Dissais
Longeville-sur-Mer
Jard-sur-Mer
La Tranche-sur-Mer
La Faute-sur-Mer
L'Aiguillon-sur-Mer
St-Michel-en-l'Herm
Triaize
Luçon
Les Landes-Genusson
La Gaubretière
La Verrie
St-Laurent-sur-Sèvre
Mont des Alouettes
Les Herbiers
Les Épesses
Sèvre Nantaise
St-Fulgent
Le Boupère
Pouzauges
Puy Crapaud
Mouchamps
Les Essarts
Montournais
Chantonnay
Bournezeau
La Châtaigneraie
La Caillère-St-Hilaire
Ste-Hermine
L'Hermenault
Fontenay-le-Comte
Nalliers
Le Langon
Chaillé-les-Marais
Vix
Maillezais
Marans
Lay
Pertuis Breton
Pte des Baleines
Pte de l'Aiguillon
Anse de l'Aiguillon
A U N I S
St-Martin-de-Ré
Ars-en-Ré
La Couarde-sur-Mer
Le Bois-Plage-en-Ré
Île de Ré
La Pallice
Rivedoux-Plage
St-Xandre
Lagord
Dompierre-sur-Mer
La Rochelle
Aytré
Angoulins
La Jarrie
Aigrefeuille-d'Aunis
Nuaillé-d'Aunis
Courçon
Pertuis d'Antioche
Pte de Chassiron
St-Denis-d'Oléron
Châtelaillon-Plage
Île d'Aix
Muron
Fouras
Port-des-Barques
Breuil-Magné
Rochefort
Tonnay-Charente
Charente
St-Georges-d'Oléron
St-Pierre-d'Oléron
Dolus-d'Oléron
Île d'Oléron
Le Château-d'Oléron
Bourcefranc-le-Chapus
St-Agnant
St-Trojan-les-Bains
Marennes
St-Just-Luzac
Ronce-les-Bains
La Tremblade
Étaules
Pte de la Coubre
Vaux-sur-Mer
St-Palais-sur-Mer
Saujon
Médis
Royan
St-Georges-de-Didonne
Semussac
Pte de Grave
Cozes
Arces
Le-Verdon-sur-Mer
Meschers-sur-Gironde
Talmont
Mortagne-sur-Gironde
Soulac-sur-Mer
Talais
Grayan-et-l'Hôpital
St-Vivien-de-Médoc
Vensac
Gironde
Montalivet-les-Bains
Vendays-Montalivet
Queyrac
Bégadan
Gallian-en-Médoc
Lesparre-Médoc
St-Germain-d'Esteuil
Naujac-sur-Mer
Vertheuil
M É D
Hourtin-Plage
Hourtin
Pauillac
St-Julien-Beychevelle
St-Laurent-Médoc
Étang d'Hourtin et de Carcans
Carcans-Plage
Listrac-Médoc
A83
E03
E601
E602
A837
N137
N160
N148
N11
N149
N215
N150
D948
D753
D937
D949
D746
D939
D911
D733
D728
D734
D26

POITOU
Plaines et Seuil du Poitou
BRANDES
CONFOLENTAIS
ANGOUMOIS
SAINTONGE
DOUBLE
PÉRIGORD BLANC
Bressuire
Parthenay
Niort
St-Maixent-l'École
Poitiers
Châtellerault
Chauvigny
Montmorillon
Le Blanc
Bellac
Confolens
Limoges
St-Junien
Ruffec
Civray
Melle
St-Jean-d'Angély
Cognac
Jarnac
Angoulême
La Rochefoucauld
Barbezieux-St-Hilaire
Jonzac
Nontron
Brantôme
Ribérac
Périgueux
Thiviers
Châlus
Rochechouart
Le Dorat
Mirebeau
Loudun
Lusignan
Vivonne
Gençay
Couhé
Chef-Boutonne
Aulnay
Matha
Pons
Archiac
Montendre
Montlieu-la-Garde
Montguyon
Chalais
Aubeterre-sur-Dronne
Montmoreau-St-Cybard
Villebois-Lavalette
Mansle
Aigre
Montbron
Chabanais
Lussac-les-Châteaux
L'Isle-Jourdain
Availles-Limouzine
Mézières-sur-Issoire
Bussière-Poitevine
Lussac-les-Églises
Mézières-en-Brenne
Thouars
Airvault
Thénezay
Vouillé
Neuville-de-Poitou
Jaunay-Clan
Dangé-St-Romain
Ingrandes
La Roche-Posay
Yzeures-sur-Creuse
St-Savin
Valdivienne
Champdeniers-St-Denis
Secondigny
Mazières-en-Gâtine
Celles-sur-Belle
Brioux-sur-Boutonne
Sauzé-Vaussais
Villefagnan
Hiersac
Châteauneuf-sur-Charente
Segonzac
Blanzac-Porcheresse
Mareuil
Verteillac
St-Aulaye
St-Astier
St-Yrieix-la-Perche
Nexon
Oradour-sur-Glane
Oradour-sur-Vayres
St-Laurent-sur-Gorre
Aixe-sur-Vienne
Monts de Châlus
A10
A83
A89
A20
E05
E62
E603
E606
E70
N10
N11
N141
N147
N149
N150
N151
N21
N145
N137
N89
25
32
37
4
5
6
A
B
C
D

Châtillon-sur-Indre
St-Flovier
Clion
Palluau-sur-Indre
St-Genou
Buzançais
Levroux
Issoudun
Charost
Civray
St-Florent-sur-Cher
Lunery
Levet
Dun-sur-Auron
Preuilly-sur-Claise
Azay-le-Ferron
Coussay-les-Bois
Yzeures-sur-Creuse
Martizay
Mézières-en-Brenne
Villedieu-sur-Indre
Niherne
Vendœuvres
St-Maur
Déols
Châteauroux
Neuvy-Pailloux
Mareuil-sur-Arnon
Châteauneuf-sur-Cher
Chezal-Benoît
La Roche-Posay
Tournon-St-Martin
BRENNE
Le Poinçonnet
Ambrault
St-Août
Lignières
Bruère-Allichamps
Orval
Angles-sur-l'Anglin
Pouligny-St-Pierre
Méobecq
Ardentes
Arthon
Pierre-de-Maillé
Matours
Le Blanc
Ruffec
St-Gaultier
Tendu
BOISCHAUT
Nohant-Vic
Le Châtelet
Thenay
Argenton-sur-Creuse
St-Marcel
Neuvy-St-Sépulchre
Montgivray
Vicq-Exemplet
Saulzais-le-Potier
St-Savin
Bélâbre
Cluis
St-Denis-de-Jouhet
La Châtre
Châteaumeillant
Culan
Prissac
Gargilesse-Dampierre
Crevant
Ste-Sévère-sur-Indre
Vallon-en-Sully
La Trimouille
St-Benoît-du-Sault
Orsennes
Barrage d'Éguzon
Éguzon-Chantôme
Lac de Chambon
Aigurande
Lourdoueix-St-Pierre
Préveranges
Montmorillon
Chaillac
La Châtre-Langlin
Crozant
La Chapelaude
BRANDES
Lussac-les-Églises
Azerables
Plateau de la Marche
Genouillac
Boussac
Huriel
Domérat
Montluçon
Moulismes
Lathus
St-Sulpice-les-Feuilles
Dun-le-Palestel
Bonnat
Châtelus-Malvaleix
Quinssaines
Adriers
St-Agnant-de-Versillat
La Souterraine
MARCHE
Magnac-Laval
Bussière-Poitevine
Le Dorat
St-Maurice-la-Souterraine
St-Vaury
Chambon-sur-Voueize
St-Bonnet-de-Bellac
St-Étienne-de-Fursac
Le Grand-Bourg
Guéret
Jarnages
Gouzon
Évaux-les-Bains
Bellac
Châteauponsac
Bessines-sur-Gartempe
Bénévent-l'Abbaye
Ste-Feyre
COMBRAILLE
Mézières-sur-Issoire
Laurière
Ahun
Chénérailles
Lac de St-Pardoux
St-Sulpice-Laurière
Moutier-d'Ahun
Lavaveix-les-Mines
Mainsat
Razès
Barrage de la Roche-Talamie
St-Dizier-Leyrenne
Auzances
Nantiat
Monts d'Ambazac
La Jonchère-St-Maurice
Pontarion
St-Sulpice-les-Champs
Cieux
Compreignac
Ambazac
Barrage de l'Étroit
Bourganeuf
Bellegarde-en-Marche
Aubusson
Oradour-sur-Glane
Nieul
Rilhac-Rancon
St-Priest-Taurion
Sauviat-sur-Vige
Étagnac
Vallières
St-Junien
Couzeix
Le Palais-sur-Vienne
Felletin
Crocq
Verneuil-sur-Vienne
Limoges
Panazol
St-Léonard-de-Noblat
Signal du Pic
Royère-de-Vassivière
Cognac-la-Forêt
Isle
Feytiat
Barrage de Vassivière
Plateau de Gentioux
St-Laurent-sur-Gorre
Aixe-sur-Vienne
Peyrat-le-Château
Gentioux-Pigerolles
Giat
Séreilhac
Plateau du Limousin
Lac de Vassivière
Châteauneuf-la-Forêt
Eymoutiers
Faux-la-Montagne
Cussac
Monts de Châlus
Pierre-Buffière
Linards
La Courtine
Nexon
Monts du Limousin
Sornac
Châlus
Mont Gargan
St-Germain-les-Belles
Plateau de Millevaches
Merlines
Bussière-Galant
Ladignac-le-Long
Bugeat
LIMOUSIN
Mialet
Meuzac
Chamberet
Mont de Bessou
La Coquille
Masseret
Treignac
Meymac
Ussel
Chaleix
St-Yrieix-la-Perche
Coussac-Bonneval
St-Angel
Jumilhac-le-Grand
Glandon
Suc-au-May
Thiviers
Angoisse
Payzac
Lubersac
Uzerche
Chamboulive
Arnac-Pompadour
Égletons
Neuvic
Bort-les-Orgues
Lanouaille
Vigeois
Seilhac
Corrèze
Barrage de Neuvic
St-Mesmin
Juillac
St-Clément
Champagnac
Coulaures
Excideuil
Salagnac
Eyrein
Cherveix-Cubas
Voutezac
Naves
St-Germain-les-Vergnes
Barrage de l'Aigle
Tourtoirac
Hautefort
Tulle
Marcillac-la-Croisille
Cubjac
Ste-Orse
Ayen
Objat
Allassac
Donzenac
Laguenne
La Roche-Canillac
Mauriac
Antonne-et-Trigonant
Badefols-d'Ans
Malemort-sur-Corrèze
Salins
Boulazac
Villac
Terrasson-Lavilledieu
Varetz
Brive-la-Gaillarde
Barrage du Chastang
Salers
Thenon
Le Lardin-St-Lazare
Larche
Beynat
St-Privat
Pleaux
St-Pierre-de-Chignac
St-Martin-Valmeroux
26
31
38

27
34
39
4
5
6
A
B
C
D
AUTUNOIS
BOURBONNAIS
Plaines de la Loire et de l'Allier
CHAROLLAIS
BRIONNAIS
Roannais
LIMAGNE
Monts de la Madeleine
Monts du Beaujolais
Plaine du Forez
Monts du Forez
Monts du Lyonnais
Monts du Livradois
MASSIF
VELAY
Monts d'Auvergne
Monts Dore
Forêt de Tronçais
Bois Noirs
Nevers
Nérondes
La Guerche-sur-l'Aubois
Gimouille
Imphy
St-Benin-d'Azy
Anlezy
Magny-Cours
La Machine
Blet
Chalivoy-Milon
Thaumiers
Sancoins
St-Parize-le-Châtel
St-Pierre-le-Moûtier
Decize
St-Léger-des-Vignes
St-Germain-Chassenay
Azy-le-Vif
Cercy-la-Tour
Vandenesse
Moulins-Engilbert
Préporché
St-Honoré-les-Bains
Villapourçon
Autun
St-Pantaléon
St-Léger-sous-Beuvray
Étang-sur-Arroux
Marmagne
Le Creusot
Mont Julien
Montcenis
Torcy
Montchanin
Sémelay
Millay
Luzy
Charbonnat
Charrin
Fours
Lanty
St-Hilaire-Fontaine
La Nocle-Maulaix
Cronat
Vitry-sur-Loire
Issy-l'Évêque
Toulon-sur-Arroux
Montceau-les-Mines
Blanzy
Mont-St-Vincent
Ainay-le-Château
Lurcy-Lévis
Couleuvre
Dornes
Lucenay-lès-Aix
Villeneuve-sur-Allier
Chevagnes
Beaulon
Bourbon-Lancy
Grury
Uxeau
Gueugnon
Perrecy-les-Forges
St-Vallier
Ciry-le-Noble
Génelard
Palinges
Marizy
Cérilly
Bourbon-l'Archambault
Avermes
Moulins
Yzeure
St-Menoux
Ygrande
Chalmoux
Neuvy-Grandchamp
Gilly-sur-Loire
Diou
Dompierre-sur-Besbre
Digoin
St-Agnan
Rigny-sur-Arroux
Martigny-le-Comte
Paray-le-Monial
St-Bonnet-de-Joux
Hérisson
Souvigny
Toulon-sur-Allier
Neuilly-le-Réal
Cosne-d'Allier
Buxières-les-Mines
Villefranche-d'Allier
Le Montet
Bessay-sur-Allier
Molinet
St-Yan
Lugny-lès-Charolles
Charolles
Changy
Dyo
Verosvres
Dompierre-les-Ormes
Jaligny-sur-Besbre
Le Donjon
Doyet
Montmarault
Commentry
St-Pourçain-sur-Sioule
Varennes-sur-Allier
Trézelles
St-Christophe-en-Brionnais
Marcigny
La Clayette
Matour
Durdat-Larequille
Chantelle
St-Gérand-le-Puy
Lapalisse
St-Prix
Urbise
Semur-en-Brionnais
Billy
Chauffailles
Montaigut
Bellenaves
St-Germain-des-Fossés
Iguerande
La Pacaudière
St-Éloy-les-Mines
Cusset
Châtel-Montagne
Briennon
Charlieu
Pouilly-sous-Charlieu
Belmont-de-la-Loire
Cours-la-Ville
Pionsat
Menat
Ébreuil
Gannat
Bellerive-sur-Allier
Vichy
Abrest
St-Yorre
Molles
Ambierle
St-Haon-le-Châtel
Lamure-sur-Azergues
St-Gervais-d'Auvergne
Aigueperse
Randan
Le Mayet-de-Montagne
Renaison
Roanne
Riorges
Le Coteau
Perreux
Bourg-de-Thizy
Amplepuis
Priest-champs
Manzat
Combronde
Thuret
Châteldon
St-Priest-la-Prugne
Villerest
Barrage de Villerest
St-Symphorien-de-Lay
Régny
Châtelguyon
St-Georges-de-Mons
Maringues
Puy-Guillaume
Puy de Montoncel
St-Just-en-Chevalet
Neulise
St-Just-la-Pendue
Tarare
Mozac
Ennezat
Riom
Volvic
St-Rémy-sur-Durolle
Chabreloche
Cremeaux
Joze
Thiers
La Monnerie-le-Montel
Néronde
Violay
Tour Matagrin
Pontgibaud
Cébazat
Gerzat
Lezoux
Peschadoires
St-Germain-Laval
Balbigny
Panissières
Chamalières
Aulnat
Pont-du-Château
Noirétable
Nervieux
Puy de Dôme
Royat
Clermont-Ferrand
Lempdes
Cournon-d'Auvergne
Courpière
Boën
Feurs
St-Laurent-de-Chamousset
Billom
Sail-sous-Couzan
Montagne
St-Amant-Tallende
Les Martres-de-Veyre
St-Dier-d'Auvergne
Olliergues
St-Georges-en-Couzan
Virigneux
Montrond-les-Bains
Ste-Foy-l'Argentière
Orcival
Aydat
Veyre-Monton
Vic-le-Comte
Pierre-sur-Haute
Chazelles-sur-Lyon
St-Sauves-d'Auvergne
St-Nectaire
St-Amant-Roche-Savine
Job
Montbrison
Savigneux
Moingt
St-Galmier
Murol
Champeix
Sauxillanges
Mont-Dore
Puy de Sancy
Issoire
Ambert
St-Anthème
Sury-le-Comtal
Bonson
Veauche
St-Héraud
La Grand-Croix
Sorbiers
Besse-et-St-Anastaise
Leiranoux
St-Germain-Lembron
Auzat-sur-Allier
St-Germain-l'Herm
Marsac-en-Livradois
Viverols
St-Just-St-Rambert
St-Bonnet-le-Château
Villars
St-Étienne
Roche-la-Molière
L'Étrat
Unieux
La Ricamarie
Jumeaux
Auzon
Arlanc
Dore-l'Église
Estivareilles
Usson-en-Forez
Aurec-sur-Loire
Firminy
Le Chambon-Feugerolles
Marchal
Condat
Anzat-le-Luguet
Le Luguet
Ardes
Lempdes
Vergongheon
Champagnac-le-Vieux
La Chaise-Dieu
Craponne-sur-Arzon
St-Pal-de-Chalancon
Tiranges
Bas-en-Basset
Monistrol-sur-Loire
St-Genest-Malifaux
Marlhes
Blesle
Lamothe
Brioude
Sembadel
Félines
Chomelix
Beauzac
St-Didier-en-Velay
Marcenat
Massiac
Vieille-Brioude
Bellevue-la-Montagne
St-Maurice-de-Lignon
St-Pal-de-Mons
Dunières
Molompize
Allanche
Villeneuve-d'Allier
St-Georges-d'Aurac
Allègre
Vorey
Retournac
Montfaucon-en-Velay
Neussargues-Moissac
La Chapelle-Laurent
Lavoûte-Chilhac
Céaux-d'Allègre
Fix-St-Geneys
St-Paulien
Lavoûte-sur-Loire
Yssingeaux
Rosières
St-Jeures
Tence
Montregard
St-Bonnet-le-Froid
Dienne
Murat
Vissac-Auteyrac
Col de la
Allier
Loire
Sioule
Dore
Arroux
Besbre
Canal latéral à la Loire
Canal du Berry
Canal de Roanne à Digoin
Aumance
Acolin
Mesvrin
Arconce
Aix
Vizézy
Alagnon
Senouire
Cronce

28
33
40
Le Creusot
Montceau-les-Mines
Montchanin
Blanzy
St-Vallier
Paray-le-Monial
Charolles
Chalon-sur-Saône
Chagny
St-Marcel
Tournus
Louhans
Cuiseaux
Lons-le-Saunier
Poligny
Arbois
Champagnole
Orgelet
St-Claude
Oyonnax
Nantua
Bellegarde-sur-Valserine
Mâcon
Cluny
La Clayette
Bourg-en-Bresse
Ambérieu-en-Bugey
Villefranche-sur-Saône
Belleville
Beaujeu
Tarare
Lyon
Villeurbanne
Vaulx-en-Velin
Bron
St-Priest
Vénissieux
Oullins
St-Fons
Rillieux-la-Pape
Meximieux
Montluel
Givors
Vienne
Bourgoin-Jallieu
Villefontaine
St-Étienne
St-Chamond
Rive-de-Gier
Firminy
Annonay
La Tour-du-Pin
Voiron
Chambéry
Aix-les-Bains
Belley
Culoz
Rumilly
Grenoble
Meylan
St-Égrève
Fontaine
Sassenage
Échirolles
CHAROLLAIS
MÂCONNAIS
BRESSE
DOMBES
BUGEY
VIGNOBLE
Lyonnais
Beaujolais
Plateau de Chambaran
Massif de la Chartreuse
Lac du Bourget
Lac de Vouglans
Lac de Paladru
A6
A39
A40
A42
A43
A47
A48
A49
A404
A432
A7
A72
E15
E21
E62
E70
E607
E611
E711
E713

Neuchâtel
Murtensee
Kerzers
Wohlen
Zollikofen
Bolligen
Ostermundigen
BERN
Muri
Worb
Köniz
Belp
Münsingen
MITTELLAND
Konolfingen
Eggiwil
Schwarzenburg
Riggisberg
Seftigen
Uetendorf
Steffisburg
Thun
Oberhofen
Hohgant
Spiez
Thuner See
Interlaken
Wimmis
Reichenbach
Lauterbrunnen
Frutigen
Männlifluh
2652
Adelboden
Blümlisalp
3664
Kandersteg
BERNER ALPEN
Balmhorn
3709
Kippel
Bietschhorn
3934
Leukerbad
CH
Lenk
Gstaad
Saanen
Zweisimmen
Simmental
Boltigen
Jaun
Charmey
Broc
Bulle
Gruyères
Le Moléson
2002
Vanil Noir
2389
Château-d'Oex
La Tornette
2540
Gsteig
Wildhorn
3248
Les Diablerets
3210
Montana
Crans-sur-Sierre
Sierre
Leuk
Raron
Chippis
Chalais
Vissoie
Stalden
Sion
Conthey
Ardon
Leytron
Vex
Nendaz
Riddes
Saxon
Evolène
Weisshorn
4505
Saas Fee
Mischabel
Matterhorn
4478
Zermatt
Täsch
Dent Blanche
4357
Arolla
Lac des Dix
Mauvoisin
Rosablanche
3336
BAGNES
Val des Bagnes
Verbier
Charrat
Sembrancher
Martigny
Champex
Orsières
Grand Combin
4314
Alpi Pennine
Monte Rosa
Breuil-Cervinia
Grande Tournalin
3379
Valtournenche
Champoluc
Gressoney-la-Trinité
Brusson
Valpelline
Monte Faroma
3073
Bionaz
Grand St Bernard
Etroubles
Gignod
Monte Fallère
3061
Aosta
St-Christophe
Nus
Châtillon
St-Vincent
Montjovet
Monte Nery
3076
Verrès
Issogne
Arnad
Fenis
Charvensod
Monte Emilius
3559
Gressan
Aymavilles
Sarre
St-Pierre
Cogne
Monte Glacier
3188
Hône
Donnas
Pont-St-Martin
Quincinetto
Settimo Vittone
Ivrea
Valsavarenche
Rhêmes-Notre-Dame
Rhêmes-St-Georges
Gran Paradiso
4061
PARCO NAZIONALE DEL GRAN PARADISO
Campiglia Soana
Monte Giavino
2766
Ronco Canavese
Noasca
Lago Serru
Locana
Pont-Canavese
Castellamonte
Cuorgnè
Valperga
Ceresole Reale
Lago di Ceresole
Orco
Groscavallo
Forno Alpi Graie
Cantoira
Ala di Stura
Ceres
CANAVESE
Rivarolo Canavese
Lanzo Torinese
Mathi
Ciriè
Cafasse
Fiano
Volpiano
Caselle Torinese
Leinì
Chivasso
Venaria
Settimo Torinese
Usseglio
Margone
Punta Lunella
2772
Stura di Viù
Bussoleno
Susa
Borgone Susa
Condove
Balme
Croix-Rousse
3541
Uia di Ciamarella
3676
L'Albaron
3637
Bonneval-sur-Arc
Pointe de Charbonnel
3752
Col du Mont Cenis
Lanslebourg-Mont-Cenis
Termignon
Dent Parrachée
3697
Grand Roc Noir
3582
PARC NATIONAL DE LA VANOISE
Pointe de la Grande Casse
3852
Pralognan-la-Vanoise
Val-d'Isère
Col de l'Iseran
Tignes
Lac du Chevril
Barrage de Tignes
Aiguille de la Grande Sassière
Mont Pourri
3779
Ste-Foy-Tarentaise
Lago di Beauregard
Valgrisenche
Becca du Lac
Col du Petit St-Bernard
La Thuile
Pre-St-Didier
Courmayeur
Morgex
La Salle
Mont Blanc
4808
Grandes Jorasses
4208
Grande Rochère
3326
St-Rhémy
Chamonix-Mont-Blanc
Aiguille du Midi
3842
Les Houches
Aiguilles des Glaciers
3816
Les Contamines-Montjoie
Mont Dolent
3823
Aiguille Verte
4122
Aiguille d'Argentière
3900
Argentière
Vallorcine
Col de la Forclaz
Vernayaz
St-Maurice
Dents du Midi
3257
Champéry
Monthey
Collombey
Bex
Ollon
Aigle
Leysin
Villeneuve
Montreux
Vevey
Châtel-St-Denis
Oron-la-Ville
Lausanne
Renens
Morges
St-Prex
Cully
Epalinges
Bussigny
Cossonay
Echallens
Moudon
Romont
Fribourg
Marly
Plaffeien
Lac de la Gruyère
La Roche
La Berra
1719
Corbières
Riaz
Düdingen
Tafers
Villars-sur-Glâne
Payerne
Avenches
Murten
Laupen
Estavayer-le-Lac
Lac de Neuchâtel
Yverdon
Yvonand
Thierrens
Peseux
Colombier
Bevaix
Les Ponts-de-Martel
Travers
Couvet
Môtiers
Fleurier
Le Chasseron
1607
Les Fourgs
La Cluse-et-Mijoux
Pontarlier
Doubs
Arçon
Le Grand Taureau
1323
Larmont
Montbenoît
Bians-les-Usiers
Levier
Frasne
Lac de St-Point
Malbuisson
Bonnevaux
Mignovillard
Mont de St-Sorlin
1237
Métabief
Le Mont d'Or
1460
Jougne
Ste-Croix
Grandson
Mont Suchet
1588
Orbe
Romainmôtier
Vallorbe
Lac de Joux
L'Abbaye
Le Sentier
Mont Tendre
1679
Vallée de Joux
Mont Risoux
Mouthe
Bière
Aubonne
Bois-d'Amont
Les Rousses
St-Cergue
La Dôle
1677
Rolle
Nyon
Divonne-les-Bains
LAC LÉMAN
Yvoire
Sciez
Thonon-les-Bains
Publier
Évian-les-Bains
Lugrin
Meillerie
St-Gingolph
Bouveret
Vouvry
Les Cornettes de Bise
2432
Vacheresse
La Chapelle-d'Abondance
Abondance
Châtel
Mont de Grange
2433
Le Biot
Bellevaux
Chablais
Douvaine
Allinges
Versoix
Veigy-Foncenex
Bons-en-Chablais
St-Cergues
Genève
Annemasse
Gaillard
Fillinges
Roc d'Enfer
2244
Les Gets
Montriond
Avoriaz
Morzine
St-Jeoire
Mieussy
Taninges
Samoëns
FAUCIGNY
Reignier
Salève
La Roche-sur-Foron
Bonneville
Thyez
Cluses
Le Cheval Blanc
3047
Sixt-Fer-à-Cheval
Le Mont Buet
3099
Flaine
St-Pierre-en-Faucigny
Scionzier
Magland
Arenthon
Pointe Percée
2752
Bornes
Le Grand-Bornand
St-Jean-de-Sixt
Sallanches
Passy
Le Brévent
2526
Servoz
Combloux
St-Gervais-les-Bains
Megève
Mont Joly
2525
Praz-sur-Arly
Flumet
Notre-Dame-de-Bellecombe
La Clusaz
Thônes
Col des Aravis
1486
Argonay
Annecy-le-Vieux
Annecy
Seynod
Talloires
La Tournette
2351
Doussard
Faverges
Ugine
Queige
Beaufort
Barrage de Roselend
Albertville
Pointe d'Arcalod
2217
Gilly-sur-Isère
La Bâthie
Le Grand Mont
2687
Le Roignais
2999
Bonneval
Bourg-St-Maurice
Séez
Isère
Les Arcs
Grésy-sur-Isère
Mont Bellacha
2483
Cevins
Feissons-sur-Isère
Aime
Beaufortin
TARENTAISE
Aiguebelle
Chamoux-sur-Gelon
Aiguelanche
Argentine
Moûtiers
Brides-les-Bains
Bozel
Courchevel
La Plagne
Épierre
Le Cheval Noir
2832
Méribel-les-Allues
St-Martin-de-Belleville
La Rochette
St-François-Longchamp
La Chambre
Massif de la Vanoise
Aiguille de Péclet
3561
St-Jean-de-Maurienne
Les Menuires
Puy Gris
2908
Col de la Croix de Fer
St-Sorlin-d'Arves
St-Michel-de-Maurienne
MAURIENNE
Arc
Modane
Aiguille de Scolette
3506
Fréjus
Pic de l'Étendard
3468
Aiguilles d'Arves
Mont Thabor
Lac du Mont Cenis
Valle di Susa
I
A
B
C
D
4
5
6
29
41
E25
E27
E62
E25/62
E27/62
E23/25
A40
A41
A43
A430
A5
N90
N212
N506
N508
N203
N5
N206
N6
E70

1
2
3
30
A
B
C
D
43
Golfe de Gascogne
Golfo de Gascuña
Gironde
Mortagne
Talais
Grayan-et-l'Hôpital
St-Vivien-de-Médoc
Vensac
Montalivet-les-Bains
Vendays-Montalivet
N215
Queyrac
Bégadan
Gallian-en-Médoc
D101
Lesparre-Médoc
D204
Naujac-sur-Mer
Vertheuil
MÉDOC
Hourtin-Plage
Hourtin
St-Laurent-Médoc
Étang d'Hourtin et de Carcans
Carcans-Plage
Carcans
Maubuisson
Listrac-Médoc
Brach
Castelnau-de-Médoc
Lacanau-Océan
Lacanau
Étang de Lacanau
Ste-Hélène
Saumos
Le Porge-Océan
Le Porge
St-Médard-en-J
Le Temple
Lège-Cap-Ferret
Arès
Andernos-les-Bains
D106
Bassin d'Arcachon
Île aux Oiseaux
Arcachon
Lanton
Audenge
Marcheprime
Biganos
Le Teich
N250
Cap Ferret
La Teste-de-Buch
Gujan-Mestras
Mios
A63
Eyre
Dune du Pilat
D218
D652
Salles
Étang de Cazaux et de Sanguinet
Sanguinet
Lugos
Biscarrosse-Plage
D146
D46
Biscarrosse
Étang de Biscarrosse et de Parentis
Parentis-en-Born
Ychoux
Gastes
Liposthey
E05/E70
Ste-Eulalie-en-Born
Pontenx-les-Forges
St-Paul-en-Born
Lüe
Canteloupe
Mimizan-Plage
Mimizan
Labouheyre
N10
Bias
Escource
Solférino
D44
Contis-Plage
Mézos
Onesse-et-Laharie
PAYS DE BORN
St-Julien-en-Born
Uza
Lit-et-Mixe
Lévignacq
D38
Morcenx
St-Girons-Plage
Lesperon
Vielle-St-Girons
Linxe
D42
Rion-des-Landes
Léon
Taller
Moliets-et-Maa
Castets
Laluque
Messanges
Azur
Herm
D947
Bégaar
Vieux-Boucau-les-Bains
Magescq
Pontonx-sur-l'Adour
N124
Soustons
St-Paul-lès-Dax
St-Vincent-de-Paul
D79
Tosse
St-Geours-de-Maremne
Narrosse
Dax
Hinx
Saubusse
Capbreton
E05/70
Bénesse-Maremne
Labenne
St-Jean-
St-Lon-
Pouillon
Pomarez

31
38
44
4
5
6
A
B
C
D
DOUBLE
PÉRIGORD BLANC
PÉRIGORD
PÉRIGORD NOIR
ENTRE-DEUX-MERS
GRAVES
PAYS
Agenais
LOMAGNE
ARMAGNAC
LANDES DE GASCOGNE
Bordeaux
Floirac
Talence
Léognan
Libourne
St Emilion
Coutras
Mussidan
Périgueux
Boulazac
Trélissac
Chancelade
Brantôme
Bourdeilles
Ribérac
Montpon-Ménestérol
Bergerac
Sarlat-la-Canéda
Le Bugue
Lalinde
Le Buisson-de-Cadouin
Beaumont
Eymet
Monpazier
Castillonnès
Villeréal
Monflanquin
Fumel
Villeneuve-sur-Lot
Ste-Livrade-sur-Lot
Penne-d'Agenais
Marmande
Tonneins
Aiguillon
Damazan
Casteljaloux
Nérac
Agen
Le Passage
Boé
Valence
Moissac
Lectoure
Condom
Fleurance
Auch
Eauze
Nogaro
Barcelone-du-Gers
Aire-sur-l'Adour
St-Sever
Mont-de-Marsan
St-Pierre-du-Mont
Roquefort
Captieux
Bazas
Langon
St-Macaire
La Réole
Sauveterre-de-Guyenne
Ste-Foy-la-Grande
Castillon-la-Bataille
Podensac
Cadillac
Barsac
Créon
Cenon
Lormont
Bassens
St-André-de-Cubzac
Bourg
Blaye
Étauliers
Mirambeau
Barbezieux-St-Hilaire
Montguyon
Chalais
Aubeterre-sur-Dronne
Mareuil
Montagrier
Tocane-St-Apre
St-Astier
Sorges
Savignac-les-Églises
Rouffignac
Vergt
Villamblard
Le Fleix
Duras
Miramont-de-Guyenne
Lauzun
Seyches
Casseneuil
Pujols
Laroque-Timbaut
Puymirol
Astaffort
Layrac
Mauvezin
Gimont
Vic-Fezensac
Montréal
Gondrin
Cazaubon
Gabarret
Houeillès
Mézin
Lavardac
Barbaste
Labrit
Brocas
Sore
Luxey
Villandraut
Préchac
Hostens
St-Symphorien
Le Tuzan
La Brède
Castres-Gironde
Portets
Saucats
Cabanac-et-Villagrains
Isle
Dronne
Dordogne
Lot
Garonne
Dropt
Ciron
Baïse
Gers
Séoune
Barguelonne
Auvézère
Ajat
A10
A62
A89
A65
E05
E70
E72
E606
N10
N21
N89
N113
N124
N134
N137
D933
D936
D939
D8
D655
D656
D931
D932
D934

1
2
3
A
B
C
D
32
37
45
Jumilhac-le-Grand
Glandon
Angoisse
Payzac
Arnac-Pompadour
Lubersac
Uzerche
Chamboulive
Suc-au-May
Égletons
St-Angel
Neuvic
Bort-les-Orgues
Lanouaille
St-Mesmin
Vigeois
Seilhac
Barrage de Neuvic
Champagnac
Ydes
St-Pierre-de-Côle
Sorges
Coulaures
Excideuil
Juillac
Salagnac
Voutezac
St-Clément
Eyrein
Savignac-les-Églises
Cherveix-Cubas
St-Germain-les-Vergnes
Naves
Tulle
Barrage de l'Aigle
Menet
Riom-ès-Montagnes
Tourtoirac
Hautefort
Objat
Allassac
Marcillac-la-Croisille
Cubjac
Ste-Orse
Ayen
Donzenac
Laguenne
Mauriac
Vallée du Falgoux
Antonne-et-Trigonant
Badefols-d'Ans
Villac
Malemort-sur-Corrèze
La Roche-Canillac
Barrage du Chastang
Salins
Périgueux
Boulazac
Ajat
Terrasson-Lavilledieu
Varetz
Brive-la-Gaillarde
Roche de Vic
Salers
Blanc
Thenon
Le Lardin-St-Lazare
Larche
Beynat
St-Privat
Pleaux
St-Martin-Valmeroux
Massif du Cantal
St-Pierre-de-Chignac
Coly
Collonges-la-Rouge
Argentat
Maronne
Barrage d'Enchanet
Rouffignac
Montignac
Plazac
Meyssac
St-Cernin
Cendrieux
Salignac-Eyvignes
Cressensac
La Chapelle-aux-Saints
Mercœur
Jussac
St-Simon
Ste-Alvère
Journiac
Causse de Martel
Beaulieu-sur-Dordogne
Siran
Laroquebrou
Le Bugue
Les Eyzies-de-Tayac-Sireuil
Borrèze
Martel
Vayrac
Biars-sur-Cère
Naucelles
Aurillac
Campagne
Sarlat-la-Canéda
Carlux
Souillac
Puybrun
Bretenoux
Teyssieu
Sansac-de-Marmiesse
Arpajon-sur-Cère
St-Cyprien
Beynac-et-Cazenac
Cazoulès
Pinsac
Montvalent
St-Céré
Sousceyrac
Ségala du Quercy
Le Buisson-de-Cadouin
Carsac-Aillac
Masclat
Lacave
Miers
Padirac
Le Rouget
Cère
Châtaigneraie
Dordogne
Cénac-et-St-Julien
Domme
Payrac
Rocamadour
Alvignac
Parlan
Belvès
St-Martial-de-Nabirat
Gourdon
Gramat
Aynac
Molières
Latronquière
Terrou
Leyme
Double Noir
Daglan
Quézac
Ladinhac
St-Pompont
Salviac
Haut Quercy
Le Bourg
Lacapelle-Marival
Maurs
Calvinet
Montsalvy
Monpazier
Mazeyrolles
St-Chamarand
Concorès
Montfaucon
Causse de Gramat
St-Constant
Cassaniouze
Villefranche-du-Périgord
Cazals
Labastide-Murat
Livernon
Assier
Cardaillac
Bagnac-sur-Célé
Biron
St-Germain-du-Bel-Air
Lamothe-Cassel
Figeac
Viazac
Grande-Vabre
Sauveterre-la-Lémance
Frayssinet-le-Gélat
Catus
Lauzès
Béduer
Capdenac
Flagnac
Conques
Lacapelle-Biron
Cuzorn
Puy-l'Évêque
Francoulès
Marcillac-sur-Célé
Capdenac-Gare
Decazeville
Firmi
Viviez
Aubin
Villecomtal
Fumel
Montayral
Monsempron-Libos
St-Vite
Mercuès
St-Géry
Cabrerets
Cajarc
Gréalou
Montbrun
Montbazens
Rodelle
Marcillac-Vallon
Salles-la-Source
Mauroux
Luzech
Pradines
Cahors
Calvignac
St-Cirq-Lapopie
Limogne-en-Quercy
Villeneuve
Sauzet
Tournon-d'Agenais
Concots
Causse de Limogne
Lanuéjouls
Compolibat
Rignac
Onet-le-Château
Rodez
Olemps
St-Pantaléon
L'Hospitalet
Lalbenque
Vaylats
Varaire
Villefranche-de-Rouergue
La Bastide-l'Évêque
Aveyron
Belcastel
Colombiès
Montaigu-de-Quercy
Montcuq
St-Cyprien
Castelnau-Montratier
St-Projet
La Rouquette
Rieupeyroux
Luc
Roquecor
Beauville
Touffailles
Belfort-du-Quercy
Puylaroque
Parisot
Baraqueville
Bourg-de-Visa
St-Maurin
Lauzerte
Cazes-Mondenard
Montpezat-de-Quercy
Caylus
Rouergue
Calmont
Séoune
Montesquieu
Molières
Verfeil
Najac
La Fouillade
La Salvetat-Peyralès
Naucelle
Castelsagrat
Bas Quercy
Monteils
Septfonds
St-Antonin-Noble-Val
Cassagnes-Bégonhès
Lamagistère
Moissac
Caussade
Réalville
Mirabel
Laguépie
Mirandol-Bourgnounac
Puech de Rouet
La Selve
Valence
Lafrançaise
Meauzac
L'Honor-de-Cos
Montricoux
Cazals
Forêt de la Grésigne
Pampelonne
Auvillar
St-Nicolas-de-la-Grave
Albias
Nègrepelisse
Penne
Vaour
Cordes
Monestiés
Carmaux
Moularès
Lédergues
Caumont
Castelsarrasin
Montauban
Vaïssac
Bruniquel
Réquista
Montbeton
Cahuzac-sur-Vère
Cagnac-les-Mines
Valderiès
Valence-d'Albigeois
Poupas
Lavit
Montech
Bressols
St-Nauphary
Castelnau-de-Montmiral
Senouillac
Lescure-d'Albigeois
Larrazet
Labastide-St-Pierre
Beaumont-de-Lomagne
Finhan
Villebrumier
Salvagnac
Marssac-sur-Tarn
Albi
Villefranche-d'Albigeois
Nohic
Gaillac
Brens
Puygouzon
Alban
Lomagne
Verdun-sur-Garonne
Fronton
Villemur-sur-Tarn
Montans
Fréjairolles
Albigeois
Canals
Grisolles
Rabastens
Lisle-sur-Tarn
Teillet
Solomiac
Aucamville
Castelnau-d'Estrétefonds
Bouloc
Coufouleux
Parisot
Labouttarie
Le Masnau-Massuguiès
Cox
Grenade
Bessières
Buzet-sur-Tarn
St-Sulpice
Giroussens
Réalmont
St-Pierre-de-Trivisy
Mauvezin
Launac
St-Jory
Bruguières
Montastruc-la-Conseillère
Briatexte
Graulhet
Cologne
Cadours
Merville
Castelginest
Fiac
Vénès
Viane
Touget
Montaigut-sur-Save
Aussonne
Beauzelle
St-Jean
Lautrec
Montredon-Labessonnié
Vabre
Lévignac
Blagnac
L'Union
Verfeil
Roquecourbe
Lacrouzette
L'Isle-Jourdain
Colomiers
Toulouse
Balma
Cap-de-Joux
St-Paul-Cap-de-Joux
Burlats
Brassac
Pibrac
Bourg-St-Bernard
Vielmur-sur-Agout
Castres

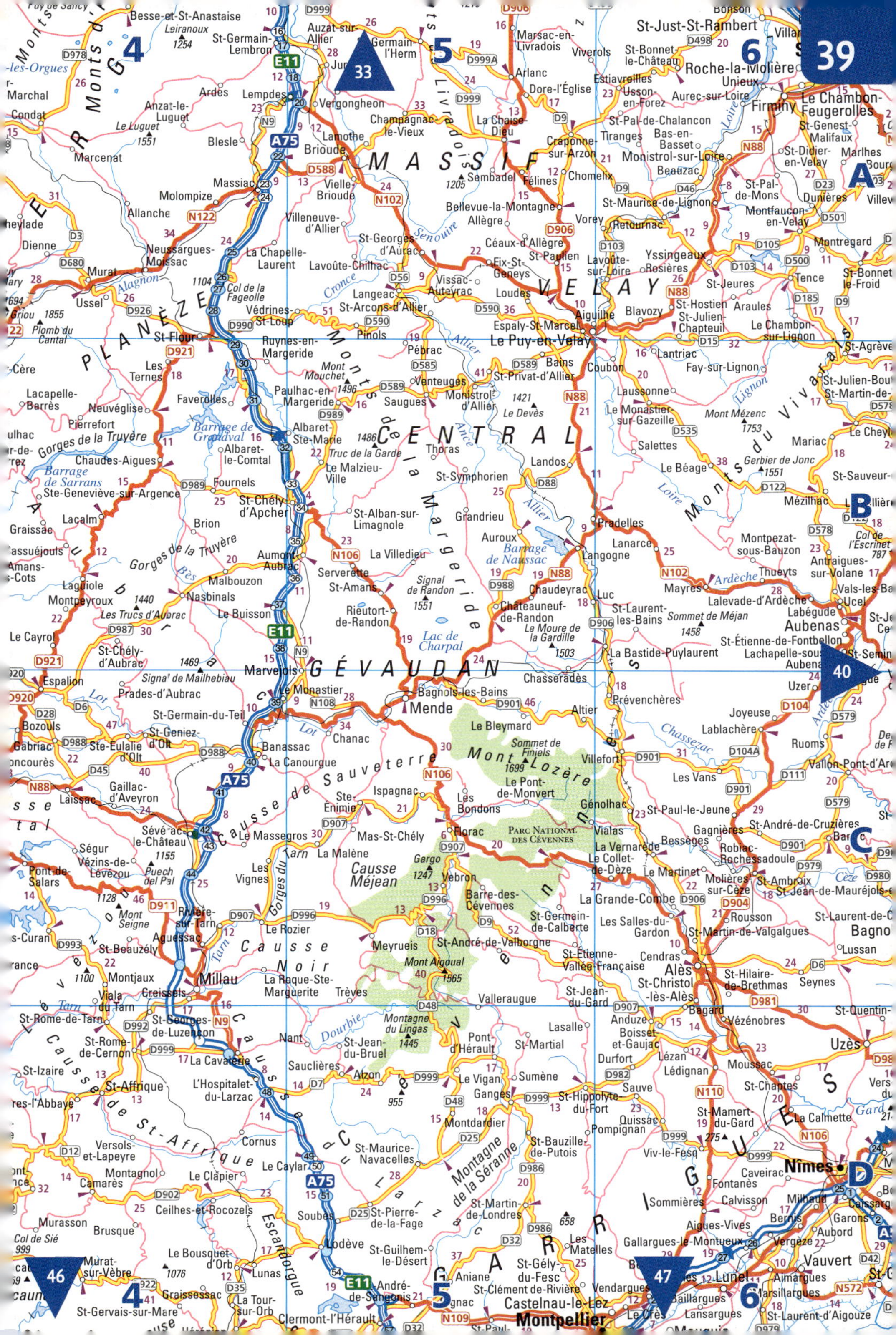
Besse-et-St-Anastaise
Leiranoux 1254
St-Germain-Lembron
Auzat-sur-Allier
Germain-l'Herm
Marsac-en-Livradois
Viverols
St-Just-St-Rambert
St-Bonnet-le-Château
Roche-la-Molière
Unieux
Firminy
Le Chambon-Feugerolles
St-Genest-Malifaux
Ardes
Lempdes
Vergongheon
Champagnac-le-Vieux
Arlanc
Dore-l'Église
Estivareilles
Usson-en-Forez
Aurec-sur-Loire
Anzat-le-Luguet
Le Luguet 1551
Blesle
Lamothe
Brioude
MASSIF
La Chaise-Dieu
Craponne-sur-Arzon
St-Pal-de-Chalancon
Tiranges
Bas-en-Basset
Monistrol-sur-Loire
Beauzac
St-Didier-en-Velay
Marlhes
Condat
Marcenat
Massiac
Vieille-Brioude
1205
Sembadel
Félines
Chomelix
St-Pal-de-Mons
Dunières
Molompize
Allanche
Villeneuve-d'Allier
Bellevue-la-Montagne
Allègre
St-Maurice-de-Lignon
Retournac
Vorey
Montfaucon-en-Velay
Montregard
Dienne
Murat
Neussargues-Moissac
La Chapelle-Laurent
Lavoûte-Chilhac
St-Georges-d'Aurac
Senouire
Céaux-d'Allègre
Fix-St-Geneys
St-Paulien
Lavoûte-sur-Loire
Yssingeaux
Rosières
Tence
St-Bonnet-le-Froid
Ussel
Alagnon
Col de la Fageolle
Cronce
Langeac
Vissac-Auteyrac
Loudes
VELAY
St-Jeures
St-Hostien
Araules
Plomb du Cantal 1855
Vèdrines-St-Loup
St-Arcons-d'Allier
Espaly-St-Marcel
Aiguilhe
Blavozy
St-Julien-Chapteuil
Le Chambon-sur-Lignon
PLANÈZE
St-Flour
Ruynes-en-Margeride
Pinols
Pébrac
Le Puy-en-Velay
Lantriac
St-Agrève
Les Ternes
Mont Mouchet 1496
Venteuges
Bains
St-Privat-d'Allier
Coubon
Fay-sur-Lignon
St-Julien-Boutières
St-Martin-de-Valamas
Lacapelle-Barrès
Faverolles
Paulhac-en-Margeride
Saugues
Monistrol-d'Allier
1421
Le Devès
Laussonne
Neuvéglise
Pierrefort
Barrage de Grandval
Albaret-Ste-Marie
CENTRAL
Le Monastier-sur-Gazeille
Mont Mézenc 1753
Gorges de la Truyère
Albaret-le-Comtal
1486
Truc de la Garde
Thoras
Salettes
Mariac
Le Cheylard
Chaudes-Aigues
Barrage de Sarrans
Le Malzieu-Ville
Landos
Gerbier de Jonc 1551
Le Béage
Ste-Geneviève-sur-Argence
Fournels
St-Chély-d'Apcher
St-Symphorien
Loire
Monts du Vivarais
St-Sauveur-de-Montagut
Mézilhac
Lacalm
St-Alban-sur-Limagnole
Grandrieu
Margeride
Graissac
Brion
Allier
Pradelles
Montpezat-sous-Bauzon
Col de l'Escrinet 787
Gorges de la Truyère
Aumont-Aubrac
La Villedieu
Auroux
Barrage de Naussac
Lanarce
Langogne
Antraigues-sur-Volane
Laguiole
Malbouzon
Serverette
St-Amans
Signal de Randon 1551
Chaudeyrac
Mayres
Ardèche
Thueyts
Vals-les-Bains
Montpeyroux
1440
Les Trucs d'Aubrac
Nasbinals
Le Buisson
Rieutort-de-Randon
Châteauneuf-de-Randon
Luc
St-Laurent-les-Bains
Lalevade-d'Ardèche
Labégude
Ucel
Aubenas
Le Cayrol
St-Chély-d'Aubrac
Lac de Charpal
Le Moure de la Gardille 1503
Sommet de Méjan 1458
St-Étienne-de-Fontbellon
Lachapelle-sous-Aubenas
Espalion
1469
Signal de Mailhebiau
Marvejols
GÉVAUDAN
La Bastide-Puylaurent
Chasseradès
Prades-d'Aubrac
Le Monastier
Bagnols-les-Bains
Mende
Altier
Prévenchères
Uzer
St-Germain-du-Teil
Lot
Chanac
Le Bleymard
Joyeuse
Lablachère
Chassezac
Bozouls
St-Geniez-d'Olt
Ste-Eulalie-d'Olt
Gabriac
Banassac
La Canourgue
Sommet de Finiels 1699
Mont Lozère
Villefort
Les Vans
Ruoms
Vallon-Pont-d'Arc
Gaillac-d'Aveyron
Causse de Sauveterre
Ispagnac
Le Pont-de-Montvert
Génolhac
Laissac
Ste-Énimie
Les Bondons
St-Paul-le-Jeune
St-André-de-Cruzières
Barjac
Sévérac-le-Château
Le Massegros
Mas-St-Chély
Florac
PARC NATIONAL DES CÉVENNES
Vialas
Gagnières
Bessèges
Ségur
Vézins-de-Lévézou
1155
Puech del Pal
La Malène
Les Vignes
Gorges du Tarn
Causse Méjean
Gargo 1247
Vebron
La Vernarède
Le Collet-de-Dèze
Robiac-Rochessadoule
Le Martinet
Molières-sur-Cèze
St-Ambroix
St-Jean-de-Maruéjols
Pont-de-Salars
Barre-des-Cévennes
La Grande-Combe
Rousson
1128
Mont Seigne
Rivière-sur-Tarn
Le Rozier
Meyrueis
St-Germain-de-Calberte
Les Salles-du-Gardon
St-Martin-de-Valgalgues
St-Laurent-de-Carnols
Bagnols
Aguessac
Causse Noir
St-André-de-Valborgne
St-Étienne-Vallée-Française
Cendras
Lussan
St-Beauzély
Mont Aigoual 1565
Alès
St-Christol-lès-Alès
St-Hilaire-de-Brethmas
Seynes
Montjaux
1100
Millau
La Roque-Ste-Marguerite
Trèves
St-Jean-du-Gard
Viala-du-Tarn
Creissels
Valleraugue
Bagard
St-Quentin-la-Poterie
St-Rome-de-Tarn
St-Georges-de-Luzençon
Dourbie
Montagne du Lingas 1445
Lasalle
Anduze
Boisset-et-Gaujac
Vézénobres
St-Rome-de-Cernon
Nant
St-Jean-du-Bruel
Pont-d'Hérault
St-Martial
Uzès
La Cavalerie
Sauclières
Durfort
Lézan
Moussac
St-Izaire
St-Affrique
L'Hospitalet-du-Larzac
Alzon
Le Vigan
Sumène
Lédignan
St-Chaptes
955
Ganges
St-Hippolyte-du-Fort
Sauve
St-Mamert-du-Gard
La Calmette
Causse de St-Affrique
Cornus
Montdardier
Quissac
Pompignan
Versols-et-Lapeyre
St-Maurice-Navacelles
St-Bauzille-de-Putois
Viv-le-Fesq
Nîmes
Montagnol
Le Clapier
Le Caylar
Causse du Larzac
Montagne de la Séranne
Caveirac
Camarès
Fontanès
Ceilhes-et-Rocozels
St-Pierre-de-la-Fage
St-Martin-de-Londres
Sommières
Calvisson
Milhaud
Caissargues
Murasson
Brusque
Escandorgue
Soubès
658
Aigues-Vives
Bernis
Garons
Col de Sié 999
Lodève
St-Guilhem-le-Désert
Les Matelles
Gallargues-le-Montueux
Vergèze
Aubord
Murat-sur-Vèbre
Le Bousquet-d'Orb
1076
Lunas
Aniane
St-Gély-du-Fesc
Vauvert
Graissessac
La Tour-sur-Orb
St-André-de-Sangonis
St-Clément-de-Rivière
Vendargues
Lunel
Aimargues
Marsillargues
St-Gervais-sur-Mare
Clermont-l'Hérault
Castelnau-le-Lez
Montpellier
Baillargues
Lansargues
St-Laurent-d'Aigouze
33
40
46
47
A
B
C
D
4
5
6

St-Héand
Grand-Croix
Rive-de-Gier
St-Romain-en-Gal
Vienne
Pont-Évêque
Estrablin
Bourgoin-Jallieu
Nivolas-Vermelle
St-Victor-de-Cessieu
St-André-le-Gaz
Les Abrets
Le Pont-de-Beauvoisin
Cognin
Barberaz
St-Béron
Sorbiers
L'Horme
St-Chamond
St-Jean-Bonnefonds
Condrieu
Eyzin-Pinet
Biol
Lac de Paladru
Col du Granier
St-Étienne
La Ricamarie
Pélussin
Chavanay
Mont Pilat
1432
St-Clair-du-Rhône
St-Maurice-l'Exil
Champier
St-Geoire-en-Valdaine
Les Échelles
Unieux
Firminy
Le Chambon-Feugerolles
Le Péage-de-Roussillon
Roussillon
Salaise-sur-Sanne
La Côte-St-André
Le Grand-Lemps
Apprieu
Voiron
St-Laurent-du-Pont
Massif de la Chartreuse
St-Genest-Malifaux
Col de la République
Serrières
St-Marcel-lès-Annonay
Chanas
St-Rambert-d'Albon
Beaurepaire
St-Étienne-de-St-Geoirs
Rives
Izeaux
St-Siméon-de-Bressieux
Viriville
La Buisse
Voreppe
Crolles
Le Touvet
St-Didier-en-Velay
Marlhes
Bourg-Argental
Annonay
Anneyron
Le Grand-Serre
Roybon
Tullins
Moirans
Noyarey
St-Égrève
Sassenage
Bernin
St-Ismier
Meylan
St-Pal-de-Mons
Dunières
Villevocance
Davézieux
Roiffieux
Albon
Hauterives
Plateau de Chambaran
Fontaine
Montfaucon-en-Velay
Quintenas
Sarras
Châteauneuf-de-Galaure
Vinay
St-Gervais
Grenoble
St-Martin-d'Hères
Domène
Montregard
Satillieu
St-Vallier
St-Uze
St-Barthélemy-de-Vals
St-Marcellin
Chatte
Izeron
Roche de Méaudre
1628
Autrans
Claix
Échirolles
Tence
St-Bonnet-le-Froid
Lalouvesc
St-Jeure-d'Ay
St-Victor
St-Donat-sur-l'Herbasse
St-Hilaire-du-Rosier
St-Romans
Villard-de-Lans
Varces-Allières-et-Risset
Le Pont-de-Claix
Chamrousse
Araules
St-Félicien
Tain-l'Hermitage
Crozes-Hermitage
Peyrins
Vizille
Le Chambon-sur-Lignon
Tournon-sur-Rhône
Mauves
Bourg-de-Péage
Romans-sur-Isère
Pont-en-Royans
Vif
Le Gua
Champ-sur-Drac
Le Taillefer
2857
St-Agrève
Monts du Vivarais
Lamastre
Pont-de-l'Isère
Cornas
Chatuzange-le-Goubet
La Chapelle-en-Vercors
Montagne de Lans
St-Georges-de-Commiers
Lignon
St-Julien-Boutières
St-Martin-de-Valamas
Boffres
St-Péray
St-Marcel-lès-Valence
Bourg-lès-Valence
St-Agnan-en-Vercors
Grand Armet
2792
Pierre-Châtel
Mézenc
1753
Vernoux-en-Vivarais
Guilherand
Valence
Montélier
Col de la Bataille
Monestier-de-Clermont
Le Cheylard
Mariac
Soyons
Malissard
Chabeuil
Léoncel
Puy de la Gagère
1651
Vassieux-en-Vercors
Le Grand Veymont
2341
Mont Aiguille
2086
Valbonnais
La Mure
Gerbier de Jonc
Charmes-sur-Rhône
Beauchastel
Portes-lès-Valence
Beaumont-lès-Valence
Montmeyran
La Raye
1015
Col de Rousset
1254
Alpes du Dauphiné
Clelles
Drac
St-Sauveur-de-Montagut
La Voulte-sur-Rhône
Livron-sur-Drôme
Montoison
Plan-de-Baix
Chamaloc
Mens
Mézilhac
Les Ollières-sur-Eyrieux
Le Pouzin
Allex
Grande Tête de l'Obiou
2790
Montpezat-sous-Bauzon
Col de l'Escrinet
787
Privas
Loriol-sur-Drôme
Crest
Aouste-sur-Sye
Pontaix
Ste-Croix
Die
Glandasse
Lalley
Col de la Croix-Haute
Thueyts
Antraigues-sur-Volane
Plateau du Coiron
Chomérac
Baix
Saulce-sur-Rhône
Aurel
Châtillon-en-Diois
Glandage
St-Étienne-en-Dévoluy
Dévoluy
Vals-les-Bains
Cruas
Marsanne
Saou
Drôme
Saillans
Lus-la-Croix-Haute
Col du Festre
1441
Ucel
St-Jean-le-Centenier
Meysse
St-Marcel-lès-Sauzet
Cléon-d'Andran
Massif du Diois
Recoubeau-Jansac
Luc-en-Diois
St-Julien-en-Beauchêne
La Cluse
Pic de Bure
2709
Aubenas
Lachapelle-sous-Aubenas
St-Sernin
Rochemaure
Alba-la-Romaine
Montboucher-sur-Jabron
Bourdeaux
Le Merlu Rocher
1613
BOCHAINE
Beaurières
La Faurie
Uzer
Vogüé
Villeneuve-de-Berg
Le Teil
Montélimar
La Bégude-de-Mazenc
St-Nazaire-le-Désert
Col de Cabre
Veynes
Ardèche
Viviers
Allan
Dieulefit
Bouvières
La Motte-Chalancon
Aspres-sur-Buëch
Aspremont
Montagne de Céüse
Ruoms
Dent de Rez
719
St-Montant
Donzère
Taulignan
1338
Rocher Garaux
Montagne de Miélandre
1451
Le Duffre
1757
Vallon-Pont-d'Arc
St-Remèze
La Garde-Adhémar
Grignan
Sahune
Eygues
Rémuzat
Montmorin
Serres
Barcillonnette
Bourg-St-Andéol
Pierrelatte
Grillon
Valréas
Rosans
L'Épine
St-André-de-Cruzières
St-Marcel-d'Ardèche
St-Paul-Trois-Châteaux
Vinsobres
Nyons
St-Sauveur-Gouvernet
Trescléoux
Ventavon
Eyguians
Barjac
Lapalud
Suze-la-Rousse
Visan
Tulette
Mirabel-aux-Baronnies
BARONNIES
Orpierre
Laragne-Montéglin
St-Ambroix
St-Jean-de-Maruéjols-et-Avéjan
Cèze
St-Just
Bollène
Pont-St-Esprit
Ste-Cécile-les-Vignes
Buis-les-Baronnies
Ouvèze
St-Auban-sur-l'Ouvèze
Montagne de Chamouse
1532
Chabre
Mison
Mondragon
Cairanne
Vaison-la-Romaine
St-Laurent-de-Carnols
Mornas
Uchaux
Sérignan-du-Comtat
Sablet
Malaucène
Mont Ventoux
1909
Montbrun-les-Bains
Séderon
Noyers-sur-Jabron
Sisteron
Bagnols-sur-Cèze
Piolenc
Camaret-sur-Aigues
Violès
Lussan
Orange
Vacqueyras
Aurel
Sommet de Lure
1826
Montagne de Lure
Peipin
Aubignosc
Seynes
Laudun
Jonquières
Aubignan
Bédoin
Revest-du-Bion
Connaux
Courthezon
Sarrians
Sault
St-Quentin-la-Poterie
Roquemaure
Carpentras
Mazan
Mormoiron
Monieux
St-Étienne-les-Orgues
Château-Arnoux
Uzès
St-Victor-la-Coste
Tavel
Bédarrides
Sorgues
Monteux
Malemort-du-Comtat
St-Christol
Banon
Peyruis
Ganagobie
Ongles
Pujaut
Entraigues-sur-la-Sorgue
Monts de Vaucluse
St-Pierre
1256
Simiane-la-Rotonde
Villeneuve-lès-Avignon
Vers-Pont-du-Gard
Pernes-les-Fontaines
Forcalquier
Lurs
La Calmette
Gard
Remoulins
Les Angles
Avignon
Le Pontet
Le Thor
St-Saturnin-lès-Apt
Mane
La Brillanne
Barbentane
Caumont-sur-Durance
Gordes
Roussillon
Rustrel
Gignac
St-Maime
Villeneuve
Aramon
Boulbon
L'Isle-sur-la-Sorgue
Nîmes
Bezouce
Marguerittes
Rognonas
Châteaurenard
Noves
Goult
Apt
St-Martin-de-Castillon
Reillanne
Dauphin
Volx
Beaucaire
Eyragues
Cabannes
Robion
Coulon
Céreste
Manosque
Milhaud
Caissargues
Bouillargues
Tarascon
St-Rémy-de-Provence
St-Andiol
Cavaillon
Bonnieux
Mourre Nègre
1125
Pierrevert
Bernis
Garons
Bellegarde
Plan-d'Orgon
Montagne du Lubéron
Cabrières-d'Aigues
Valensole
Vergèze
Aubord
Rhône
Canal des Alpilles
Orgon
Lourmarin
Cucuron
Ste-Tulle
Corbières
Vauvert
Fourques
Fontvieille
Alpilles
Les Opiès
493
Sénas
Lauris
Villelaure
Cadenet
Beaumont-de-Pertuis
Mirabeau
Vinon-sur-Verdon
Aimargues
St-Gilles
Arles
Aureille
Mouriès
Eyguières
Lamanon
Mallemort
Pertuis
St-Martin-de-Crau
Durance
Salon-de-Provence
39
34
47
48

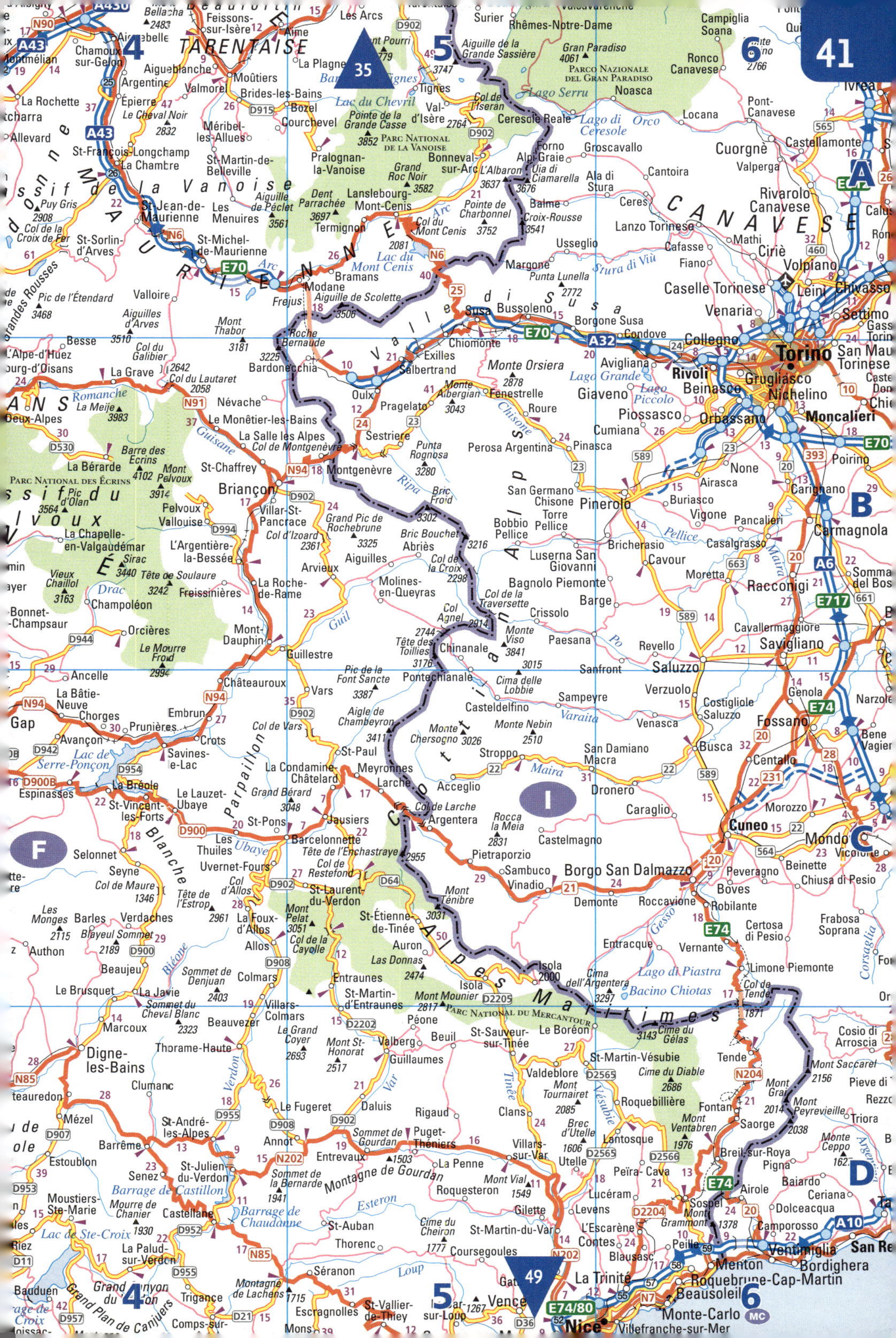
TARENTAISE
Bellacha 2483
Feissons-sur-Isère
Aime
Les Arcs
Mont Pourri 3779
Aiguebelle
Chamoux-sur-Gelon
Montmélian
La Plagne
Aiguille de la Grande Sassière
Surier
Rhêmes-Notre-Dame
Gran Paradiso 4061
PARCO NAZIONALE DEL GRAN PARADISO
Campiglia Soana
Ronco Canavese
Ivrea
Aiguebelle
Argentine
Moûtiers
Brides-les-Bains
Valmorel
Tignes
3747
Lago Serru
Noasca
Pont-Canavese
La Rochette
Épierre
Le Cheval Noir 2832
Bozel
Courchevel
Lac du Chevril
Pointe de la Grande Casse 3852
Val-d'Isère
2764
Col de l'Iseran
Ceresole Reale
Lago di Ceresole
Orco
Locana
Castellamonte
Allevard
Méribel-les-Allues
PARC NATIONAL DE LA VANOISE
Forno Alpi Graie
Groscavallo
Cuorgnè
Valperga
St-François-Longchamp
La Chambre
St-Martin-de-Belleville
Pralognan-la-Vanoise
Grand Roc Noir 3582
Bonneval-sur-Arc
L'Albaron 3637
Uia di Ciamarella 3676
Ala di Stura
Cantoira
Massif de la Vanoise
Puy Gris 2908
Col de la Croix de Fer
Aiguille de Péclet 3561
Dent Parrachée 3697
Lanslebourg-Mont-Cenis
Pointe de Charbonnel 3752
Balme
Ceres
CANAVESE
Rivarolo Canavese
St-Jean-de-Maurienne
Les Menuires
Termignon
Croix-Rousse 3541
Lanzo Torinese
Mathi
Ciriè
St-Sorlin-d'Arves
St-Michel-de-Maurienne
Col du Mont Cenis
2081
Lac du Mont Cenis
Usseglio
Cafasse
Volpiano
Fiano
MAURIENNE
Arc
Bramans
Margone
Stura di Viù
Leini
Chivasso
Valloire
Modane
Punta Lunella 2772
Caselle Torinese
Grandes Rousses
Pic de l'Étendard 3468
Aiguilles d'Arves 3510
Fréjus
Aiguille de Scolette 3506
Susa
Bussoleno
Valle di Susa
Borgone Susa
Venaria
Settimo
Mont Thabor 3181
Roche Bernaude 3225
Chiomonte
Condove
Collegno
Torino
San Mauro Torinese
Besse
Col du Galibier 2642
L'Alpe-d'Huez
Bourg-d'Oisans
Bardonecchia
Exilles
Salbertrand
Monte Orsiera 2878
Avigliana
Lago Grande
Rivoli
Grugliasco
La Grave
Col du Lautaret 2058
Oulx
Monte Albergian 3043
Fenestrelle
Giaveno
Lago Piccolo
Beinasco
Nichelino
Romanche
La Meije 3983
Névache
Pragelato
Chisone
Roure
Piossasco
Orbassano
Moncalieri
Deux-Alpes
Le Monêtier-les-Bains
Sestriere
Cumiana
La Salle les Alpes
Col de Montgenèvre
Punta Rognosa 3280
Perosa Argentina
Pinasca
Poirino
La Bérarde
Barre des Écrins 4102
Guisane
Mont Pelvoux 3914
St-Chaffrey
Montgenèvre
Airasca
None
PARC NATIONAL DES ÉCRINS
Briançon
Ripa
Bric Froid
San Germano Chisone
Pinerolo
Carignano
Massif du Pelvoux
Pic d'Olan 3564
Pelvoux
Vallouise
Villar-St-Pancrace
Grand Pic de Rochebrune 3325
3302
Torre Pellice
Buriasco
Vigone
Carmagnola
La Chapelle-en-Valgaudémar
L'Argentière-la-Bessée
Col d'Izoard 2361
Bric Bouchet
Abriès
3216
Bobbio Pellice
Pancalieri
Pellice
Casalgrasso
Sirac 3440
Tête de Soulaure 3242
Aiguilles
Col de la Croix 2298
Luserna San Giovanni
Bricherasio
Cavour
Maira
Vieux Chaillol 3163
Drac
Freissinières
La Roche-de-Rame
Arvieux
Molines-en-Queyras
Bagnolo Piemonte
Moretta
Racconigi
Champoléon
Col de la Traversette
Barge
Sommariva del Bosco
Bonnet-Champsaur
Orcières
Mont-Dauphin
Guil
Col Agnel 2744
2914
Monte Viso 3841
Crissolo
Cavallermaggiore
Savigliano
Le Mourre Froid 2994
Guillestre
Tête des Toillies 3176
Chinanale
Paesana
Po
Revello
Ancelle
Châteauroux
Pic de la Font Sancte 3387
Pontechianale
3015
Sanfront
Saluzzo
La Bâtie-Neuve
Embrun
Vars
Cima delle Lobbie
Casteldelfino
Sampeyre
Verzuolo
Costigliole Saluzzo
Genola
Gap
Chorges
Prunières
Aigle de Chambeyron 3411
Monte Chersogno 3026
Monte Nebin 2510
Varaita
Venasca
Fossano
Narzole
Avançon
Lac de Serre-Ponçon
Crots
Savines-le-Lac
Col de Vars
Parpaillon
St-Paul
Stroppo
San Damiano Macra
Busca
Centallo
Bene Vagienna
Espinasses
La Bréole
Le Lauzet-Ubaye
La Condamine-Châtelard
Meyronnes
Larche
Maira
Acceglio
Dronero
St-Vincent-les-Forts
Grand Bérard 3048
Col de Larche
Argentera
Rocca la Meia 2831
Caraglio
Morozzo
Mondovì
F
I
St-Pons
Jausiers
Castelmagno
Cuneo
Selonnet
Blanche
Les Thuiles
Ubaye
Barcelonnette
Tête de l'Enchastraye 2955
Pietraporzio
Vicoforte
Seyne
Uvernet-Fours
Col de Restefond
Sambuco
Vinadio
Borgo San Dalmazzo
Peveragno
Beinette
Col de Maure 1346
Col d'Allos
St-Laurent-du-Verdon
Mont Ténibre 3031
Demonte
Roccavione
Boves
Chiusa di Pesio
Les Monges 2115
Barles
Tête de l'Estrop 2961
La Foux-d'Allos
Mont Pelat 3051
St-Étienne-de-Tinée
Robilante
Verdaches
Blayeul Sommet 2189
Allos
Col de la Cayolle
Auron
Alpes Maritimes
Entracque
Gesso
Certosa di Pesio
Frabosa Soprana
Authon
Bléone
Las Donnas 2474
Vernante
Beaujeu
Sommet de Denjuan 2403
Colmars
Entraunes
Isola
Isola 2000
Cima dell'Argentera 3297
Lago di Piastra
Limone Piemonte
Corsaglia
Le Brusquet
La Javie
St-Martin-d'Entraunes
Mont Mounier 2817
PARC NATIONAL DU MERCANTOUR
Bacino Chiotas
Col de Tende 1871
Sommet du Cheval Blanc 2323
Villars-Colmars
Péone
Beuil
St-Sauveur-sur-Tinée
Le Boréon
Cime du Gélas 3143
Cosio di Arroscia
Marcoux
Beauvezer
Le Grand Coyer 2693
Mont St-Honorat 2517
Valberg
Thorame-Haute
Guillaumes
St-Martin-Vésubie
Tende
Digne-les-Bains
Valdeblore
Cime du Diable 2686
Mont Saccarel 2156
Pieve di Teco
Mont Tournairet 2085
Mont Gran... 2014
Rezzo
Clumanc
Verdon
Var
Tinée
Vésubie
Roquebillière
Fontan
Mont Peyrevieille 2038
Triora
Le Fugeret
Daluis
Rigaud
Clans
Brec d'Utelle 1606
Saorge
Mont Ventabren 1976
Mézel
St-André-les-Alpes
Lantosque
Monte Ceppo 1627
Barrême
Annot
Sommet de Gourdan
Puget-Théniers
Villars-sur-Var
Utelle
Breil-sur-Roya
Pigna
Estoublon
St-Julien-du-Verdon
Entrevaux
1503
La Penne
Peïra-Cava
Baiardo
Senez
Barrage de Castillon
Sommet de la Bernarde 1941
Montagne de Gourdan
Mont Vial 1549
Lucéram
Airole
Ceriana
Moustiers-Ste-Marie
Mourre de Chanier 1930
Castellane
Barrage de Chaudanne
Esteron
Roquesteron
Gilette
Levens
Sospel
Mont Grammont 1378
Dolceacqua
Lac de Ste-Croix
St-Auban
Cime du Cheiron 1777
St-Martin-du-Var
L'Escarène
Contes
Camporosso
Riez
La Palud-sur-Verdon
Thorenc
Coursegoules
Blausasc
Peille
Ventimiglia
San Remo
Séranon
Loup
La Trinité
Menton
Bordighera
Bauduen
Grand Canyon du Verdon
Trigance
Montagne de Lachens 1715
Escragnolles
St-Vallier-de-Thiey
Le Bar-sur-Loup
1267
Vence
Roquebrune-Cap-Martin
Beausoleil
Monte-Carlo
MC
Grand Plan de Canjuers
Comps-sur-Artuby
Mons
Nice
Villefranche-sur-Mer
A43
A430
N90
N6
E70
A32
A6
E717
E74
A10
E74/80
N94
N85
N202
N204
N7
D902
D915
D2205
D2202
D2565
D2566
D2204
D900
D900B
D954
D942
D530
D944
D994
D955
D952
D953
D957
D907
D908
D21
D36
D64
35
49
4
5
6
A
B
C
D

1
2
3
A
B
C
D
E
Plymouth
Portsmouth
Golfe
Golf
Cabo Mayor
Bahía de Santander
Cabo de Ajo
Cabo Machichaco
Santander
Santa Cruz de Bezana
Suances
Santillana
Muriedas
El Astillero
Torrelavega
San Miguel
Renedo
Cartes
Puente Viesgo
Luzmela
Rivero
Los Corrales de Buelna
Pomaluengo
Santa María de Cayón
San Martín
La Concha
Penagos
Valdecilla
La Cavada
Rubayo
Carriazo
Ajo
Noja
Santoña
Escalante
Beranga
Gama
Laredo
Colindres
Limpias
Solórzano
Bádames
Ampuero
El Puente
Rasines
Riba
Ramales de la Victoria
Arredondo
Villacarriedo
Selaya
Vega de Pas
San Vicente de Toranzo
Arenas de Iguña
Molledo
Bárcena de Pie de Concha
Los Pandos
San Pedro del Romeral
Barcenillas de Cerezos
Espinosa de los Monteros
Embalse del Ebro
Espinilla
Reinosa
Arija
Pedrosa
Soncillo
Nela
Puerto Pozazal
Arroyal
Mataporquera
Castro-Urdiales
Sopelana
Algorta
Santurtzi
Portugalete
Sestao
Barakaldo
Bilbao (Bilbo)
Arizgoiti
Lamiako
Erandio
Berango
Plentzia
Bakio-Basigo
Bermeo
Mundaka
Busturi-Axpe
Mungia
Murueta
Gernika-Lumo
Berriatua
Markina-Xemein
Krutzea
Zornotza
Zaratamo
Arrigorriaga
Igorre
Durango
Mañaria
Ugarana
Areatza
Zubiaur
Ceanuri-Elexondo
Baranbio
Otxandio
Ubidea
Elorrio
Mondragón-Arrasate
Aretxabaleta
Ermua
Zaldibar
Abadiño
Llodio
Amurrio
Orduña
Güeñes
Molinar
Mimetiz
Mercadillo
Balmaseda
Concha
Montes de Ordunte
Arceniega
Villasana de Mena
Arespalditza
Bercedo
Villasante de Montija
Castrobarto
Sierra Salvada
LA LOSA
Embalse de Urrúnaga
Legutiano
Murgia
Gopegi
Izarra
Durana
Embalse de Ullibarri
La Cerca
Medina de Pomar
Villarcayo
Incinillas
Marzanedo
Boveda
Osma
Zuazo de Cuartango
Langraiz Oka
Vitoria-Gasteiz
Salinas de Añana
Villanueva de Valdegovia
Quintana-Martín Galíndez
Nofuentes
Trespaderne
Sierra de la Tesla
Puerto de la Mazorra
Dobro
Polientes
Pesadas de Burgos
Sedano
Tubilla del Agua
LA LORA
Basconcillos del Tozo
Aguilar de Campóo
Ebro
Frías
Embalse de Sobrón
Oña
Cornudilla
Montes Obarenes
Poza de la Sal
Cubo de Bureba
Pancorbo
Miranda de Ebro
Zambrana
CONDADO DE TREVIÑO
Treviño
Montes de Vitoria
La Puebla de Arganzón
Berantevilla
Peñacerrada
Lagran
Sierra de Cantabria
Cernégula
Masa
Quintana del Pino
Puerto del Páramo de Masa
Sotresgudo
LA BUREBA
Briviesca
Rublacedo de Abajo
Treviana
Villalba de Rioja
San Vicente de la Sonsierra
Haro
Briones
Laguardia
Elciego
Cenicero
Fuenmayor
Logroño
Tirgo
Casalarreina
Castañares de Rioja
San Asensio
Herramélluri
Cerezo de Riotirón
Santo Domingo de la Calzada
Hormilla
Villadiego
Huérmeces
Santibáñez Zarzaguda
Urbel
Villegas
Sasamón
Villanueva de Argaño
Puerto de la Brújula
Alcocero de Mola
Quintanapalla
Villaescusa la Sombría
Belorado
Villafranca-Montes de Oca
Nájera
Villar de Torre
Navarrete
Alesón
Sotés
Albelda de Iregua
Badarán
Baños de Río Tobía
Sotopalacios
Rubena
Burgos
Tardajos
Buniel
Villasandino
Castrojeriz
Estepar
Arcos
Cardeñadijo
Sarracín
Ibeas de Juarros
Arlanzón
Villasur de Herreros
Pradoluengo
Ezcaray
San Millán de la Cogolla
Pedroso
Anguiano
Sierra de la Demanda
Revilla del Campo
Pineda de la Sierra
Sierra de San Lorenzo
Pedrosa del Príncipe
Pampliega
Cogollos
Hontoria de la Cantera
Cuevas de San Clemente
Santa María del Campo
Villahizán
Madrigal del Monte
Palenzuela
Villahoz
Covarrubias
Hortigüela
Barbadillo del Pez
Barbadillo de Herreros
Mansilla
Villavelayo
Viniegra de Arriba
Ortigosa
Villanueva de Cameros
Pradillo
Montenegro de Cameros
Lumbreras
Sierra de Neila
Arlanzón
A67
A8
E70
A68
E804
A1
E05
E80
A231

36
44
Golfe de Gascogne
Golfo de Gascuña
Côte d'Argent
PAYS BASQUE
RIBERA NAVARRA
BÁRDENAS REALES
CINCO VILLAS
Sierra de Aralar
Sierra de Andía
Sierra de Urbasa
Sierra de Lóquiz
Sierra de Urquilla
Sierra de Abodi
Sierra de Labia
Sierra de Izco
Sierra de Santo Domingo
Sierra de Luna
Puerto de Velate
Puerto de Ibañeta
Puerto Echegárate
Col d'Ispéguy
Embalse de Yesa
Adour
Ebro
Aragón
Arga
Ega
F
Vielle-St-Girons
Linxe
Rion-des-Landes
Léon
Castets
Taller
Laluque
Moliets-et-Maa
Messanges
Azur
Herm
Vieux-Boucau-les-Bains
Soustons
Magescq
Bégaar
Tartas
Pontonx-sur-l'Adour
Audon
Souprosse
St-Paul-lès-Dax
St-Vincent-de-Paul
Mugron
Montaut
Gamarde-les-Bains
Narrosse
Tosse
St-Geours-de-Maremne
Dax
Hinx
Montfort-en-Chalosse
Soorts-Hossegor
Œyreluy
Saubusse
Bastennes
Capbreton
Bénesse-Maremne
Labenne
St-Jean-de-Marsacq
St-Lon-les-Mines
Pouillon
Pomarez
St-Cricq-Chalosse
Amou
Ondres
Tarnos
Biarrotte
Habas
Tilh
Puyôo
Sault-de-Navailles
Peyrehorade
Boucau
St-Martin-de-Seignanx
Sorde-l'Abbaye
Hagetaubin
Bayonne
St-Pierre-d'Irube
Urt
Bidache
Orthez
Biarritz
Anglet
Bardos
Bidart
Arcangues
Briscous
Escos
Salies-de-Béarn
Villefranque
La Bastide-Clairence
Sauveterre-de-Béarn
Lagor
St-Jean-de-Luz
Ciboure
Urrugne
Larressore
Ustaritz
Hasparren
Luxe-Sumberraute
Montfort
Bugnein
Noguères
Hondarribia
St-Pée-sur-Nivelle
Cambo-les-Bains
Mourenx
Hendaye
Ascain
St-Esteben
Castetnau-Camblong
Navarrenx
Donostia - San Sebastián
Pasai Donibane
Irun
Sare
Espelette
St-Palais
Zumaia
Getaria
Zarautz
Orio
Errenteria
Lasarte
Elizalde
Bera de Bidasoa
Lesaka
Urdax-Urdazuli
Iholdy
Irissarry
Lucq-de-Béarn
Zestoa
Zubieta
Andoain
Hernani
Urnieta
Zizurkil
Etxalar
St-Martin-d'Arrossa
Ossès
Larceveau-Arros-Cibits
Chéraute
Mauléon-Licharre
Azpeitia
Villabona
Arano
Amaiur-Maia
St-Étienne-de-Baïgorry
Ispoure
St-Just-Ibarre
Mendite
Barcus
Azkoitia
Errezil
Anoeta
Goizueta
Sunbilla
Donezteben
Elizondo
Irurita
St-Jean-Pied-de-Port
Tardets-Sorholus
Aramits
Tolosa
Ibarra
Oronoz
Arnéguy
Alçay-Alçabéhéty-Sunharette
Zumarraga
Leitza
Ezkurra
Aldudes
Montory
Arette
Ordizia
Amezketa
Urepel
Haux
Sarrance
Beasain
Lazkao
Idiazabal
San Martín
Betelu
Lekunberri
Larrau
Orreaga
Auritz
Ste-Engrâce
Arette-Pierre-St-Martin
Altsasu
Etxarri-Aranatz
Lakuntza
Uharte-Arakil
Irurtzun
Jauntsarats
Olague
Lintzoain
Zubiri
Garralda
Aribe
Orbara
Ochagavía
Lescun
Lizarraga
Olazti
Ostiz
Erice
Olave
Larrasoaina
Escároz
Jaurrieta
Esparza de Salazar
Isaba
Zunzarren
Nagore
Ollo
Berriozar
Villava
Huarte
Burlada
Aizpún
Ororbia
Barañáin
Pamplona (Iruñea)
Vidángoz
Roncal
Güesa
Zudaire
Echarri
Gazolaz
Mutilva Baja
Aoiz
Aós
Ansó
Eulate
Belascoáin
Noáin
Urroz
Irurozqui
Hecho
Larrión
Salinas de Pamplona
Elorz
Ardanaz
Burgui
Galbarra
Arizala
Estella
Cirauqui
Biurrun
Monreal
Navascués
Castillo-Nuevo
Puente la Reina
Tiebas
Idocin
Lumbier
Bigüézal
Acedo
Ancín
Villatuerta
Mañeru
Liédena
Yesa
Sigües
Biniés
Oteiza
Mendigorría
Aibar
Berdún
Santa Cilia de Jaca
Morentin
Artajona
Barásoain
Javier
Arronitz
Pueyo
Eslava
Sangüesa
Artieda
Los Arcos
Allo
Larraga
Tafalla
Navardún
Urriés
Pintano
Sansol
San Martín de Unx
Cáseda
Bailo
Lazagurría
Sesma
Lerín
Miranda de Arga
Olite
Sos del Rey Católico
Isuerre
Lobera de Onsella
Mendavia
Lodosa
Santa María
Alcanadre
Andosilla
Falces
Santacara
Murillo el Fruto
Carcastillo
Castiliscar
Biel
Murillo de Río Leza
Cárcar
Sartaguda
San Adrián
Peralta
Mélida
Uncastillo
Luesia
Ausejo
Pradejón
Caparroso
Loarre
El Villar de Arnedo
Calahorra
Azagra
Funes
Marcilla
Layana
Asín
Orés
Robres del Castillo
Bergasa
Aldeanueva de Ebro
Milagro
Sádaba
Ayerbe
Biota
Arnedo
Rincón de Soto
Cadreita
Arnedillo
Quel
Autol
Valtierra
Farasdues
Plasencia del Monte
Alfaro
Arguedas
Pinsoro
Bárdena
Luna
Valpalmas
Castejón
Ejea de los Caballeros
Enciso
Valareña
Grávalos
Corella
Igea
Cintruénigo
Tudela
El Sabinar
Alcalá de Gurrea
Las Pedrosas
Cornago
A8
E70
A15
E05/80
A63
E05/70
E05
A64
E80
N10
N124
N117
A68
E804
A15
121A
240A
D933
D932
D918
4
5
6
A
B
C
D

Mont-de-Marsan
St-Pierre-du-Mont
Villeneuve-de-Marsan
Mauléon-d'Armagnac
Bretagne-d'Armagnac
Mouchan
Gondrin
Valence-sur-Baïse
St-Puy
Terraube
Pauilhac
Fleurance
Meilhan
Tartas
Le Leuy
Benquet
Bascons
St-Gein
Panjas
Eauze
Courrensan
Lannepax
Castéra-Verduzan
Audon
Souprosse
Grenade-sur-l'Adour
Le Houga
Manciet
Bascous
Vic-Fezensac
St-Vincent-de-Paul
Mugron
Montaut
St-Sever
Montsoué
Duhort-Bachen
Aire-sur-l'Adour
Nogaro
Dému
Jegun
Puycasquier
Gamarde-les-Bains
Montfort-en-Chalosse
Eugénie-les-Bains
Barcelonne-du-Gers
Aignan
St-Jean-Poutge
Preignan
Ordan-Larroque
Bastennes
Hagetmau
Geaune
St-Germé
Riscle
ARMAGNAC
Lupiac
Le Brouilh-Monbert
Auch
Pessan
Pomarez
St-Cricq-Chalosse
Samadet
Aurensan
Plaisance
Beaumarchés
Montesquiou
Bassoues
L'Isle-de-Noé
Pavie
Habas
Tilh
Amou
Sault-de-Navailles
Malaussanne
Sarron
Castelnau-Rivière-Basse
Madiran
Labatut-Rivière
Marciac
Puyôo
Arzacq-Arraziguet
Méraq
Garlin
Taron-Sadirac-Viellenave
Mirande
Seissan
Saramon
Orthez
Hagetaubin
Morlanne
Arthez-de-Béarn
Mazerolles
Thèze
Maubourguet
Lembeye
Lafitole
Tillac
Salies-de-Béarn
Sauveterre-de-Béarn
Lagor
Lacq
Artix
Sauvagnon
Serres-Castet
Sévignacq
St-Laurent-Bretagne
Rabastens-de-Bigorre
Blousson-Sérian
St-Michel
Miélan
St-Elix-Theux
Masseube
Montfort
Bugnein
Noguères
Denguin
Lescar
Buros
Vic-en-Bigorre
Bazillac
Villecomtal-sur-Arros
Panassac
St-Ost
Mourenx
Pardies
Monein
Morlaàs
Montaner
Trie-sur-Baïse
Boulogne-sur-Gesse
Castetnau-Camblong
Navarrenx
Lons
Billère
Pau
Idron-Ousse-Sendets
Andrest
Bazet
Pouyastruc
Castelnau-Magnoac
Lucq-de-Béarn
Jurançon
Gelos
Bizanos
Bordères-sur-l'Échez
Aureilhan
Séméac
Blajan
Monléon-Magnoac
Lespugue
Chéraute
Mauléon-Licharre
Oloron-Ste-Marie
Lasseube
Gan
Soumoulou
Ger
Ibos
Tarbes
Juillan
Galan
Bordes
Tournay
NÉBOUZAN
Barcus
Escout
Ogeu-les-Bains
Nay-Bourdettes
Bénéjacq
Pontacq
Ossun
Laloubère
Bernac-Dessus
Houeydets
St-Plancard
Tardets-Sorholus
Asasp-Arros
Bidos
Rébénacq
Asson
Coarraze
Montaut
Montgaillard
Lannemezan
Villeneuve-de-Rivière
Aramits
Lurbe-St-Christau
Arudy
Bielle
Louvie-Juzon
Arthez-d'Asson
St-Pé-de-Bigorre
Lourdes
Bagnères-de-Bigorre
Cieutat
Capvern-les-Bains
La Barthe-de-Neste
St-Laurent-de-Neste
Montréjeau
Gourdan-Polignan
Labarthe-Rivière
Montory
Haux
Arette
Sarrance
Bedous
Accous
Laruns
Col d'Aubisque
Arbéost
Aucun
Agos-Vidalos
Argelès-Gazost
Pierrefitte-Nestalas
Campan
Hèches
St-Bertrand-de-Comminges
Valcabrère
Ste-Engrâce
St-Martin
Lescun
Gourette
Soulom
BIGORRE
Col d'Aspin
Sarrancolin
Mauléon-Barousse
Sost
Cierp-Gaud
Fronsac
St-Béat
Isaba
Urdos
Cauterets
PARC NATIONAL DES PYRÉNÉES OCCIDENTALES
Luz-Ardiden
Chèze
Barèges
La Mongie
Col du Tourmalet
Arreau
Bordères-Louron
Roncal
Candanchú
Col du Somport
Col du Pourtalet
Sallent de Gállego
Luz-St-Sauveur
Gèdre
Piau-Engaly
Aragnouet
Vielle-Aure
St-Lary-Soulan
Col de Peyresourde
Bagnères-de-Luchon
Bòssost
Col du Portillon
Ansó
Hecho
Balneario de Panticosa
Huesca
Panticosa
Gavarnie
Villanúa
Port de Venasque
Montes Malditos
Castiello de Jaca
Biescas
Torla
Broto
Fanlo
PARQUE NACIONAL ORDESA - MONTE PERDIDO
Bielsa
Benasque
Biniés
Berdún
Santa Cilia de Jaca
Jaca
Sarvisé
Sahun
Santa Cruz de la Serós
Sabiñánigo
Fiscal
Lafortunada
Castejón de Sos
Bailo
Sierra de San Juan de la Peña
Yebra de Basa
Albella
Boltaña
Santa María
Gállego
Caldearenas
Laguarta
Ainsa
Campo
Pont de Suert
Sierra de Santo Domingo
Sierra de Javierre
Aquilué
Molino de Villobas
Embalse de Mediano
CONDADO
Loarre
Arguis
Arcusa
Sopeira
Ayerbe
Bolea
Rodellar
Santa Liestra y San Quílez
Nueno
Sierra de Guara
Arén
Plasencia del Monte
Aguas
Barcabo
Embalse de El Grado
Luna
Lupiñén
Naval
Graus
Lascuarre
Valpalmas
Alerre
Bierge
El Grado
Puente de Montañana
Embalse de Sotonera
Huesca
Adahuesca
Erla
Angüés
Abiego
Canal de Cinca
Olvena
Tolva
Benabarre
Alcalá de Gurrea
Blecua
Peraltilla
Barbastro
Sierra de Carrodilla
Embassament de Canelles
Las Pedrosas
Almudévar
Albero Alto
SOMONTANO
Estadilla
SOBRARBE
BÉARN
CONDOM
PYRÉNÉES

Beaumont-de-Lomagne
Verdun-sur-Garonne
Finhan
Nohic
Villebrumier
Fronton
Salvagnac
Gaillac
Brens
Montans
Puygouzon
Fréjairolles
Lisle-sur-Tarn
Parisot
Coufouleux
Bessières
Buzet-sur-Tarn
St-Sulpice
Giroussens
Laboutarie
Graulhet
Briatexte
Réalmont
St-Pierre-de-Trivisy
Le Masnau-Massuguiès
Vénès
Montredon-Labessonnié
Vabre
Viane
Solomiac
Aucamville
Castelnau-d'Estréfonds
Grisolles
Canals
Cox
Launac
Grenade
St-Jory
Bouloc
Bruguières
Montastruc-la-Conseillère
Mauvezin
Cadours
Merville
Castelginest
Lavaur
Fiac
Lautrec
Roquecourbe
Burlats
Lacrouzette
Brassac
Le Bez
Cologne
Montaigut-sur-Save
Lévignac
Aussonne
Beauzelle
St-Jean
L'Union
Verfeil
Blagnac
Colomiers
Balma
Bourg-St-Bernard
St-Paul-Cap-de-Joux
Vielmur-sur-Agout
Castres
Lagarrigue
Boissezon
Anglès
L'Isle-Jourdain
Pibrac
Toulouse
Tournefeuille
St-Orens-de-Gameville
Lanta
Cuq-Toulza
Puylaurens
Saïx
Soual
Payrin-Augmontel
Sidobre
Plaisance-du-Touch
Fontenilles
Fonsorbes
Cugnaux
Portet-sur-Garonne
Ramonville-St-Agne
Castanet-Tolosan
Caraman
Blan
Labruguière
Aussillon
Mazamet
Pont-de-Larn
Labastide-Rouairoux
St-Lys
Seysses
Villeneuve-Tolosane
Samatan
Ste-Foy-de-Peyrolières
Baziège
Revel
Dourgne
Sorèze
Arfons
St-Amans-Soult
Lombez
Lherm
Muret
Vernet
Montgiscard
St-Félix-Lauragais
Les Cammazes
Montagne Noire
Lespinas
Rieumes
Eaunes
Villefranche-de-Lauragais
Lauragais
Saissac
Cuxac-Cabardès
Mas-Cabardès
Caunes-Minervois
Montpézat
Bérat
Longages
Lagardelle-sur-Lèze
Gardouch
Labastide-d'Anjou
St-Papoul
Castelnaudary
Lastours
Gratens
Noé
Auterive
Nailloux
St-Sulpice-sur-Lèze
Cintegabelle
Le Fousseret
St-Élix-le-Château
Carbonne
Cujac
Calmont
Salles-sur-l'Hers
Fendeille
Villepinte
Moussoulens
Conques-sur-Orbiel
Peyriac-Minervois
Villemoustaussou
Alzonne
Pennautier
Carcassonne
Trèbes
La Redorte
Mondavezan
Rieux
Lézat-sur-Lèze
St-Ybars
Mazères
Villasavary
Bram
Canal du Midi
Aurignac
St-Julien
Cazères
Montesquieu-Volvestre
Saverdun
Montaut
Belpech
Montréal
Lavalette
Cazilhac
Floure
Martres-Tolosane
Le Vernet
Fanjeaux
Preixan
Leuc
Montlaur
Le Plan
Le Fossat
Artigat
Pamiers
Belvèze-du-Razès
Ste-Croix-Volvestre
Daumazan-sur-Arize
Sabarat
La Tour-du-Crieu
Mirepoix
Alaigne
Lauraguel
St-Hilaire
Salies-du-Salat
Mane
Fabas
Le Mas-d'Azil
Pailhès
St-Jean-du-Falga
Verniolle
La Bastide-de-Bousignac
Moulin-Neuf
Limoux
St-Pierre-des-Champs
Caumont
Clermont
Varilhes
Alet-les-Bains
Plateau de Lecamp
Montagnes du Plantaurel
Dun
Laroque-d'Olmes
Aigues-Vives
Léran
St-Benoît
Arbas
St-Lizier
St-Girons
Rimont
La Bastide-de-Sérou
Montels
Foix
Chalabre
Arques
Engomer
Lacourt
Massif de l'Arize
Montgaillard
Lavelanet
La Bastide-sur-l'Hers
Puivert
Espéraza
Couiza
Rennes-les-Bains
Castillon-en-Couserans
Biert
St-Paul-de-Jarrat
Montferrier
Bélesta
Nébias
Quillan
Corbières
Soulatgé
Bethmale
Soueix
Massat
Saurat
Arignac
Montségur
Ginoles
Caudiès-de-Fenouillèdes
Seix
Oust
Tarascon-sur-Ariège
Belcaire
Espezel
Ustou
Aulus-les-Bains
Prades
Axat
St-Paul-de-Fenouillet
Couflens
Vicdessos
Auzat
Les Cabannes
Luzenac
Port de Pailhères
Pays de Sault
Escouloubre
Sournia
Port de Salau
Ascou
Salardu
Alós d'Ensil
Ax-les-Thermes
Quérigut
Ille-sur-Têt
Esterri d'Aneu
Mérens-les-Vals
Molitg-les-Bains
Vinça
Marquixanes
El Serrat
L'Hospitalet-près-l'Andorre
Formiguères
Prades
AND
Arinsal
Soldeu
Les Angles
Conflent
Vernet-les-Bains
Espot
Parc Nacional d'Aigües Tortes i Estany de Sant Maurici
Escaló
Col de Puymorens
Olette
St-Marsal
La Massana
Encamp
Port d'Envalira
Porta
Font-Romeu-Odeillo-Via
Thuès-entre-Valls
Mont-Louis
Andorra la Vella
Les Escaldes
Llavorsí
Llívia
Planès
Sant Julià de Lòria
Puigcerdà
Saillagouse-Llo
La Torre de Cabdella
Rialp
Ger
Osséja
La Preste
Prats-de-Mollo-la-Preste
Sort
Le Seu d'Urgell
Martinet
Bellver de Cerdanya
Alp
Queralbs
Molló
Vilallonga
Camprodon
Guerri de la Sal
Serra del Cadí
Ribes de Freser
Sant Joan de les Abadesses
Sant Joan les Fonts
La Pobla de Segur
Serra del Boumort
Bagà
La Pobla de Lillet
Coll de Merolla
Guardiola de Berguedà
Ripollès
Campdevànol
Ripoll
Olot
Organyà
Serra de Querol
Sant Privat d'en Bas
Tremp
Pantà de la Baells
Vilada
Alpens
Les Preses
Berga
Avià
Sant Llorenç de Morunys
Sant Quirze de Besora
Sant Agustí de Lluçanès
Sant Pere de Torelló
Sant Feliu de Pallerols
Isona
Berguedà
Olvan
Torelló
Peramola
Oliana
Castellnou
Castellar de la Ribera
Gironella
Perafita
Santa Maria

Frejairolles
Teillet
38
Réalmont
Graulhet
Briatexte
Fiac
Agout
Lautrec
Vénès
Montredon-Labessonnié
Vabre
Roquecourbe
Burlats
Lacrouzette
Vielmur-sur-Agout
Castres
Lagarrigue
Boissezon
Saïx
Soual
Puylaurens
Blan
Labruguière
Payrin-Augmontel
Aussillon
Mazamet
Pont-de-Larn
St-Amans-Soult
Sidobre
Dourgne
Revel
Sorèze
Arfons
Montagne Noire
Les Cammazes
Le Masnau-Massuguiès
Viane
Lacaune
Col de Sié
Monts de Lacaune
Brassac
Le Bez
Anglès
La Salvetat-sur-Agout
Labastide-Rouairoux
Col de la Fenille
Belmont-sur-Rance
Versols-et-Lapeyre
Montagnol
Camarès
Murasson
Brusque
Murat-sur-Vèbre
Monts de l'Espinouse
Olargues
Mons
Riols
St-Pons-de-Thomières
Col de Rodomouls
St-Gervais-sur-Mare
Graissessac
Hérépian
Lamalou-les-Bains
Cornus
Le Clapier
Le Caylar
Ceilhes-et-Rocozels
Escandorgue
Le Bousquet-d'Orb
Lunas
La Tour-sur-Orb
Bédarieux
Clermont-l'Hérault
St-Maurice-Navacelles
Soubès
Lodève
St-Pierre-de-la-Fage
St-Guilhem-le-Désert
St-André-de-Sangonis
Gignac
Canet
Faugères
Paulhan
Laurens
Roujan
Roquebrun
Cessenon-sur-Orb
Espondeilham
Pézenas
Valros
Montagnac
Villeveyrac
Hérault
Murviel-lès-Béziers
Servian
Boujan-sur-Libron
St-Thibéry
Lignan-sur-Orb
Béziers
Maraussan
Bessan
Marseillan
Vias
Agde
Villeneuve-lès-Béziers
Sérignan
Valras-Plage
Cap d'Agde
AURAGAIS
Castelnaudary
St-Papoul
Saissac
Cuxac-Cabardès
Mas-Cabardès
Lespinassière
Caunes-Minervois
MINERVOIS
Aigues-Vives
St-Chinian
Puisserguier
Cruzy
Capestang
Montady
Villepinte
Moussoulens
Lastours
Conques-sur-Orbiel
Villemoustaussou
Alzonne
Pennautier
Peyriac-Minervois
Olonzac
Argeliers
Nissan-lez-Enserune
Villasavary
Bram
Canal du Midi
Carcassonne
Trèbes
La Redorte
Lézignan-Corbières
Ginestas
Canet
Ouveillan
Cuxac-d'Aude
Coursan
Lespignan
Fleury
Villedaigne
Capendu
Moux
Ornaisons
Bizanet
Vinassan
Armissan
Narbonne
Narbonne-Plage
Fanjeaux
Belvèze-du-Razès
Montréal
Lavalette
Preixan
Cazilhac
Floure
Leuc
Montlaur
Fabrezan
Ferrals-les-Corbières
Gruissan
Mirepoix
Alaigne
Lauraguel
St-Hilaire
Limoux
St-Pierre-des-Champs
Lagrasse
St-Laurent-de-la-Cabrerisse
Portel-des-Corbières
Étang de l'Ayrolle
Sigean
Port-la-Nouvelle
Moulin-Neuf
Alet-les-Bains
Plateau de Lecamp
Aigues-Vives
St-Benoît
Léran
Villerouge-Termenès
Durban-Corbières
La Palme
Chalabre
Espéraza
Arques
Puivert
Couiza
Rennes-les-Bains
Mouthoumet
Leucate
Cap Leucate
Bélesta
Nébias
Quillan
CORBIÈRES
Tuchan
Opoul-Périllos
Fitou
Étang de Leucate ou de Salses
Ginoles
Soulatgé
Paziols
Caudiès-de-Fenouillèdes
Vingrau
Salses-le-Château
Port-Leucate
Espezel
Maury
Espira-de-l'Agly
Port-Barcarès
Axat
St-Paul-de-Fenouillet
St-Laurent-de-la-Salanque
Port de Pailhères
Pays de Sault
Escouloubre
Estagel
Latour-de-France
Baixas
Rivesaltes
Sournia
St-Estève
Bompas
Ste-Marie
Quérigut
Millas
Perpignan
Canet-en-Roussillon
Canet-Plage
Molitg-les-Bains
Ille-sur-Têt
Toulouges
Formiguères
Marquixanes
Vinça
Thuir
Corneilla-del-Vercol
Alénya
St-Cyprien
Les Angles
CONFLENT
Prades
Elne
Bages
Fourques
Vernet-les-Bains
ROUSSILLON
St-André
Argelès-sur-Mer
Collioure
Côte Vermeille
Font-Romeu-Odeillo-Via
Olette
St-Marsal
Port-Vendres
Thuès-entre-Valls
Mont-Louis
Planès
Llivia
Amélie-les-Bains-Palalda
Céret
Maureillas-las-Illas
Le Boulou
Banyuls-sur-Mer
Saillagouse-Llo
Le Perthus
Col du Perthus
Cerbère
Cap Cerbère
Portbou
Osséja
La Preste
Prats-de-Mollo-la-Preste
St-Laurent-de-Cerdans
Coustouges
La Jonquera
Agullana
Maçanet de Cabrenys
Espolla
Llançà
Queralbs
Molló
Vilallonga
Camprodon
Pantà de Boadella
El Port de la Selva
Cap de Creus
Vilajuïga
Ribes de Freser
La Pobla de Lillet
Coll de Merolla
Sant Joan de les Abadesses
Albanyà
Terrades
Peralada
Figueres
Vilafant
Cadaqués
Roses
Cap de Norfeu
Castelló d'Empúries
Campdevànol
Ripoll
Sant Joan les Fonts
Tortellà
Navata
Olot
Besalú
Fluvià
Golf de Roses
Sant Pere Pescador
Vilada
Sant Privat d'en Bas
Santa Pau
Esponellà
Serinyà
Bàscara
L'Armentera
Alpens
Les Preses
Porqueres
Viladamat
L'Escala
Cala Montgó
Sant Agustí de Lluçanès
Sant Quirze de Besora
Sant Pere de Torelló
Sierra Finestres
Mieres
Banyoles
Camallera
Colomers
Olvan
Torelló
Sant Feliu de Pallerols
Les Planes d'Hostoles
Cornellà Terri
Verges
Perafita
Sant Hipòlit de Voltregà
Manlleu
Santa Maria de Corcó
Amer
Sarrià de Ter
Bordils
Celrà
Torroella de Montgrí
A61
A9
A75
A7
E80
E15
E11
N112
N113
N116
N9
N114

Nîmes
Montpellier
Lunel
Mauguio
La Grande-Motte
Lattes
Pérols
Palavas-les-Flots
Frontignan
Mireval
Golfe d'Aigues-Mortes
Aigues-Mortes
Le Grau-du-Roi
Pointe de l'Espiguette
PETITE CAMARGUE
CAMARGUE
Vauvert
St-Gilles
Beaucaire
Tarascon
Arles
Fontvieille
Alpilles
St-Rémy-de-Provence
Châteaurenard
Cavaillon
St-Martin-de-Crau
CRAU
Étang de Vaccarès
Stes-Maries-de-la-Mer
Golfe de Stes Maries ou Beauduc
Pointe du Sablon
Salin-de-Giraud
Port-St-Louis-du-Rhône
Plage de Piémanson
Fos-sur-Mer
Port-de-Bouc
Martigues
Golfe de Fos
Cap Couronne
Sausset-les-Pins
Carry-le-Rouet
Ensuès-la-Redonne
Istres
Miramas
St-Chamas
Berre-l'Étang
Marignane
Vitrolles
Rognac
Les Pennes-Mirabeau
Salon-de-Provence
Lambesc
Pélissanne
Aix-en-Provence
Marseille
Île Pomègues
Île Ratonneau
Cap Croisette
Île Riou
Canal des Alpilles
Canal de Marseille au Rhône
Grand Rhône
Petit Rhône
Rhône
Durance
A54
E80
A7
E714
E80/714
N113
N568
N570
N572
Golfe du Lion
Alger, Annaba, Bejaïa, Skikda, Tunis
Alicante, Oran
Palma de Mallorca
39
40
48
A
B
C
D
4
5
6

40
41
47
1
2
3
A
B
C
D
F
Apt
Goult
Gignac
St-Martin-de-Castillon
Reillanne
Dauphin
St-Maime
Oraison
Villeneuve
Volx
Céreste
Manosque
Pierrevert
Valensole
Puimoisson
Moustiers-Ste-Marie
Senez
Barrage de Castillon
Castellane
Barrage de Chaudanne
Sommet de la Bernarde 1941
Mourre de Chanier 1930
La Palud-sur-Verdon
Lac de Ste-Croix
Roumoules
Riez
Asse
Mourre Nègre 1125
Montagne du Luberon
Cabrières-d'Aigues
Lourmarin
Cucuron
Lauris
Cadenet
Villelaure
Beaumont-de-Pertuis
Mirabeau
Ste-Tulle
Corbières
Gréoux-les-Bains
Vinon-sur-Verdon
Quinson
Barrage de Ste-Croix
Bauduen
Moissac-Bellevue
Grand Canyon du Verdon
Grand Plan de Canjuers
Montagne de Barjaude 1173
Trigance
Comps-sur-Artuby
Artuby
Montagne de Lachens 1715
Séranon
Escragnolles
Mons
Seillans
Callian
Fayence
Bargemon
Montferrat
Callas
Figanières
Draguignan
Trans-en-Provence
Les Arcs
Le Muy
St-Paul-en-Forêt
Mandelieu-la-Napoule
Alleins
Lambesc
Pélissanne
St-Cannat
Rognes
Pertuis
Peyrolles-en-Provence
Jouques
St-Paul-lès-Durance
Ginasservis
La Verdière
Montmeyan
Aups
Ampus
Venelles
Meyrargues
Rians
Varages
Esparron
St-Martin
Barjols
Tavernes
Sillans-la-Cascade
Salernes
Villecroze
Lorgues
Flayosc
Éguilles
La Fare-les-Oliviers
Vauvenargues
Montagne Ste-Victoire 1011
Aix-en-Provence
Velaux
Rognac
Berre-l'Étang
Vitrolles
Meyreuil
Gardanne
Rousset
Pourrières
Brue-Auriac
Cotignac
PROVENCE
Estérel
Carcès
Taradeau
Trets
Pourcieux
St-Maximin-la-Ste-Baume
Le Val
Brignoles
Cabasse
Vidauban
Roquebrune-sur-Argens
Fréjus
St-Raphaël
Marignane
St-Victoret
Les Pennes-Mirabeau
Bouc-Bel-Air
Tête du Grand Puech 781
Peynier
La Bouilladisse
Septèmes-les-Vallons
Peypin
Auriol
St-Zacharie
Nans-les-Pins
Signal de la Ste-Baume 1147
Chaîne de la Ste-Baume
Le Luc
Le Cannet-des-Maures
Besse-sur-Issole
Col de Gratteloup
Plan-de-la-Tour
Massif des Maures
Martigues
Ensuès-la-Redonne
Carry-le-Rouet
Sausset-les-Pins
Marseille
Île Pomègues
Île Ratonneau
Aubagne
Roquevaire
Gémenos
Néoules
Garéoult
Carnoules
Pignans
Gonfaron
La Garde-Freinet
Grimaud
Ste-Maxime
Golfe de St-Tropez
St-Tropez
Cap de St-Tropez
Les Issambres
Pointe des Issambres
St-Aygulf
Signes
Méounes-lès-Montrieux
Col de la Bigue 423
Jas de Laure 826
Puget-Ville
Collobrières
La Sauvette 779
Cogolin
Carnoux-en-Provence
Cuges-les-Pins
Cassis
Ceyreste
Le Castellet
Le Beausset
Solliès-Toucas
Cuers
Solliès-Pont
Pierrefeu-du-Var
La Môle
La Croix-Valmer
Ramatuelle
Cap Camarat
Cap Croisette
Île de Riou
La Ciotat
St-Cyr-sur-Mer
Bandol
Ollioules
La Valette-du-Var
La Farlède
La Crau
Rayol-Canadel-sur-Mer
Cavalaire-sur-Mer
Cap Cartaya
Sanary-sur-Mer
La Seyne-sur-Mer
Six-Fours-les-Plages
Toulon
La Garde
Hyères
La Londe-les-Maures
Le Lavandou
Rade de Bormes
Cap Bénat
Carqueiranne
Cap Sicié
Golfe de Giens
Presqu'île de Giens
Rade d'Hyères
Île du Levant
Île de Port-Cros
Parc National de Port-Cros
Île de Porquerolles
Îles d'Hyères
Alger, Annaba, Bejaia, Skikda, Tunis
Tunis
E714
E712
E80/714
E80
A7
A8
A50
A51
A57
N7
N8
N96
N97
N98
N113
N85
N560
D1
D3
D5
D6
D11
D12
D21
D23
D4
D25
D543
D552
D554
D556
D557
D558
D559
D560
D561
D562
D563
D952
D953
D955
D957
D973
D943
D554
D562

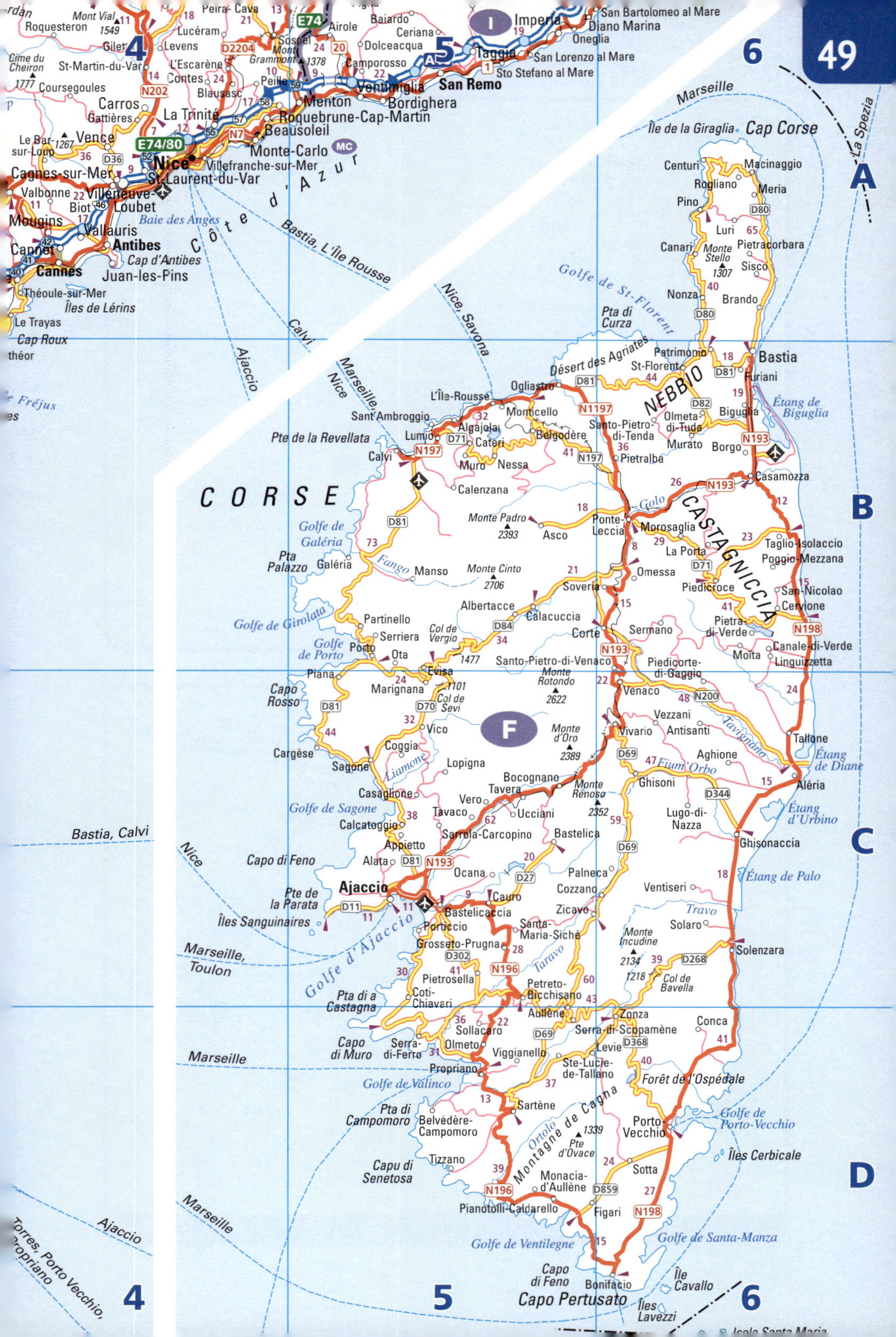
A
B
C
D
4
5
6
CORSE
F
I
MC
Cap Corse
Île de la Giraglia
La Spezia
Marseille
Centuri
Macinaggio
Rogliano
Meria
Pino
Luri
Pietracorbara
Canari
Monte Stello
1307
Sisco
Nonza
Brando
Golfe de St-Florent
Pta di Curza
Désert des Agriates
Patrimonio
Bastia
St-Florent
Furiani
NEBBIO
Étang de Biguglia
Biguglia
Ogliastro
Santo-Pietro-di-Tenda
Olmeta-di-Tuda
Murato
Borgo
Pietralba
Casamozza
L'Île-Rousse
Sant'Ambroggio
Monticello
Algajola
Belgodère
Lumio
Cateri
Pte de la Revellata
Calvi
Muro
Nessa
Calenzana
Golo
CASTAGNICCIA
Golfe de Galéria
Monte Padro
2393
Asco
Ponte-Leccia
Morosaglia
Taglio-Isolaccio
Poggio-Mezzana
La Porta
Pta Palazzo
Galéria
Fango
Manso
Monte Cinto
2706
Omessa
Piedicroce
San-Nicolao
Cervione
Soveria
Albertacce
Calacuccia
Pietra-di-Verde
Golfe de Girolata
Partinello
Serriera
Col de Vergio
Corte
Sermano
Moïta
Canale-di-Verde
Linguizzetta
Golfe de Porto
Porto
Ota
1477
Santo-Pietro-di-Venaco
Piedicorte-di-Gaggio
Piana
Evisa
Monte Rotondo
2622
Venaco
Capo Rosso
Marignana
1101
Col de Sevi
Vezzani
Antisanti
Tavignano
Tallone
Vico
Monte d'Oro
2389
Vivario
Aghione
Cargèse
Coggia
Fium'Orbo
Étang de Diane
Sagone
Liamone
Lopigna
Bocognano
Ghisoni
Aléria
Casaglione
Vero
Tavera
Monte Renoso
2352
Lugo-di-Nazza
Étang d'Urbino
Golfe de Sagone
Tavaco
Ucciani
Calcatoggio
Sarrola-Carcopino
Bastelica
Ghisonaccia
Appietto
Capo di Feno
Alata
Ocana
Palneca
Étang de Palo
Ajaccio
Cauro
Cozzano
Ventiseri
Pte de la Parata
Bastelicaccia
Zicavo
Travo
Îles Sanguinaires
Porticcio
Santa-Maria-Siché
Solaro
Golfe d'Ajaccio
Grosseto-Prugna
Monte Incudine
2134
Solenzara
Marseille, Toulon
Taravo
1218
Col de Bavella
Pietrosella
Pta di a Castagna
Coti-Chiaveri
Petreto-Bicchisano
Aullène
Zonza
Conca
Sollacaro
Serra-di-Scopamène
Capo di Muro
Serra-di-Ferro
Olmeto
Levie
Viggianello
Ste-Lucie-de-Tallano
Propriano
Forêt de l'Ospédale
Golfe de Valinco
Sartène
Montagne de Cagna
Golfe de Porto-Vecchio
Pta di Campomoro
Belvédère-Campomoro
Ortolo
1339
Pte d'Ovace
Porto-Vecchio
Îles Cerbicale
Capu di Senetosa
Tizzano
Monacia-d'Aullène
Sotta
Pianotolli-Caldarello
Figari
Golfe de Ventilegne
Golfe de Santa-Manza
Capo di Feno
Bonifacio
Île Cavallo
Capo Pertusato
Îles Lavezzi
Isola Santa Maria
Marseille
Ajaccio
Torres, Porto Vecchio, Propriano
Bastia, Calvi
Nice
Nice, Savona
Marseille, Nice
Calvi
Ajaccio
Bastia, L'Île Rousse
Côte d'Azur
Baie des Anges
Cap d'Antibes
Cannes
Juan-les-Pins
Antibes
Vallauris
Mougins
Biot
Valbonne
Villeneuve-Loubet
Cagnes-sur-Mer
Nice
St-Laurent-du-Var
Villefranche-sur-Mer
Monte-Carlo
Beausoleil
Roquebrune-Cap-Martin
Menton
La Trinité
Vence
Le Bar-sur-Loup
1267
Carros
Gattières
Coursegoules
Cime du Cheiron
1777
St-Martin-du-Var
Gilette
Levens
Roquesteron
Mont Vial
1549
Lucéram
L'Escarène
Contes
Blausasc
Peille
Peira-Cava
Sospel
Mont Grammont
1378
Airole
Baiardo
Ceriana
Dolceacqua
Camporosso
Ventimiglia
Bordighera
San Remo
Taggia
Imperia
San Bartolomeo al Mare
Diano Marina
Oneglia
San Lorenzo al Mare
Sto Stefano al Mare
Théoule-sur-Mer
Îles de Lérins
Le Trayas
Cap Roux
Fréjus
E74
E74/80
A10
D2204
N202
D36
N7
N193
N197
N1197
N198
N196
N200
D81
D80
D82
D71
D84
D70
D69
D344
D27
D11
D302
D268
D368
D859

Key to city map symbols

- E55 — Euro route number
- A13 — Motorway
- Motorway – toll
- 37 — Motorway junction – full access
- 12 — Motorway junction – restricted access
- Motorway services
- 309 — Main road – dual carriageway
- Main road – single carriageway
- 516 — Secondary road – dual carriageway
- Secondary road – single carriageway
- Other road
- Motorway tunnel
- Main road tunnel
- Motorway/road under construction
- Road toll
- International airport
- Railway
- Tunnel
- Funicular railway
- Car ferry
- 480 — Summit (height in metres)
- Canal
- International boundary
- Urban area
- Parkland
- Woodland
- Place of interest

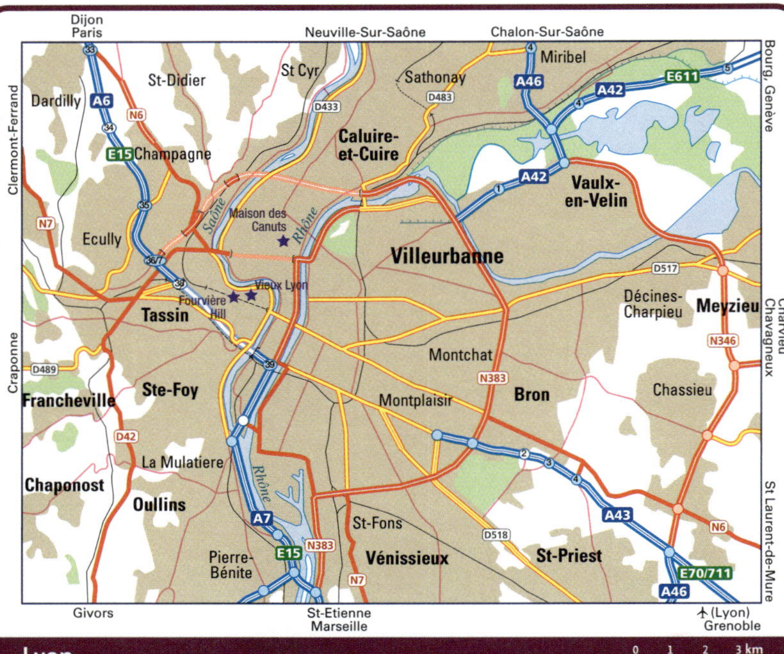

Lyon

Marseille

0 1 2 3 km

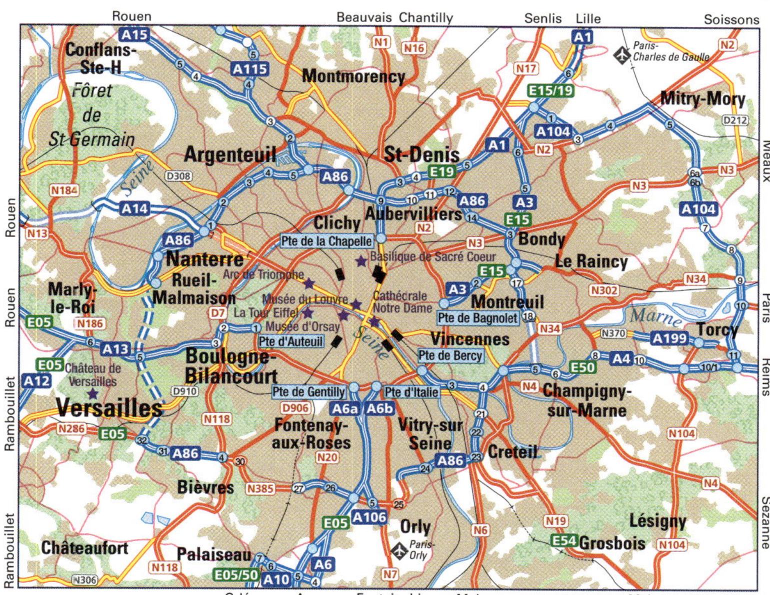

Paris

0 5 10 km

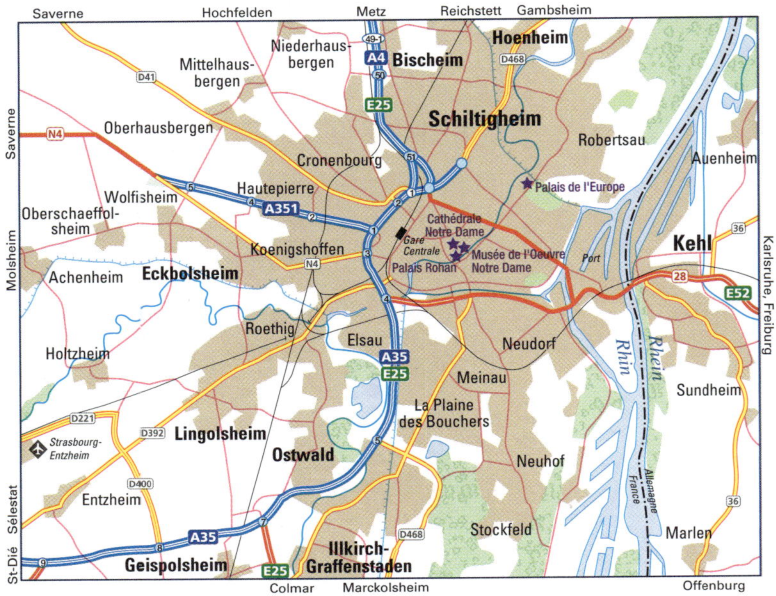

Strasbourg

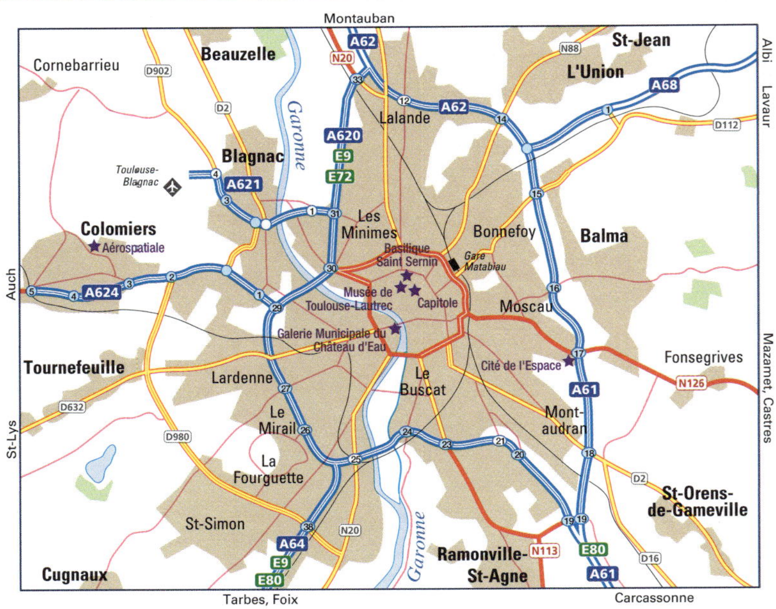

Toulouse

A

B

C

D

E

F

H

I

J

K

L

M

N

O

P

Q

R

S

W

X

Y

Z